CONVERSATIONS
WITH SCRIPTURE:
THE GOSPEL
OF JOHN

CONVERSATIONS
WITH SCRIPTURE:

THE GOSPEL
OF JOHN

CYNTHIA BRIGGS KITTREDGE

MOREHOUSE PUBLISHING

HARRISBURG NEW YORK

Unless otherwise noted, the Scripture quotations contained herein are from the New Revised Standard Version Bible, copyright © 1989 by the Division of Christian Education of the National Council of Churches of Christ in the U.S.A. Used by permission. All rights reserved.

Morehouse Publishing and the Anglican Association of Biblical Scholars thank the Louisville Institute for their interest in and support of this series.

Hymn texts quoted on pages 38, 47, 74, and 86 are from *The Hymnal 1982,* © 1985 by The Church Pension Fund. Used by permission.

Morehouse Publishing, 4775 Linglestown Road, Harrisburg, PA 17105

Morehouse Publishing, 445 Fifth Avenue, New York, NY 10016

Morehouse Publishing is an imprint of Church Publishing Incorporated.

Cover art by He Qi (www.heqigallery.com).

Series design by Beth Oberholtzer

Library of Congress Cataloging-in-Publication Data

Kittredge, Cynthia Briggs.
    Conversations with Scripture : the Gospel of John / Cynthia Kittredge.
       p. cm. — (Anglican Association of Biblical Scholars study series)
    Includes bibliographical references.
    ISBN 978-0-8192-2249-7 (pbk.)
    1. Bible. N.T. John—Criticism, interpretation, etc.   I. Title.
BS2615.52.K565   2007
226.5'06—dc22

2007021510

Printed in the United States of America

07 08 09 10 11 12   10 9 8 7 6 5 4 3 2 1

For Michael Floyd, Ray Pickett, and Steve Bishop,
Friends and Colleagues

With affection and gratitude
for our teamwork in teaching the Bible.

Holy and Loving God, who has granted us a vision of your glory, give us minds wide enough and hearts sufficiently generous to see your signs in the world you have made, and give us the will to befriend one another as you have befriended us, through Jesus Christ, your Son, Divine Wisdom, Teacher, our Lord and our God.

AMEN.

CONTENTS

INTRODUCTION
TO THE SERIES

To talk about a distinctively Anglican approach to Scripture is a daunting task. Within any one part of the larger church that we call the Anglican Communion there is, on historical grounds alone, an enormous variety. But as the global character of the church becomes apparent in ever-newer ways, the task of accounting for that variety while naming the characteristics of a distinctive approach becomes increasingly difficult.

In addition, the examination of Scripture is not confined to formal studies of the kind addressed in this series of parish studies written by formally trained biblical scholars. Systematic theologian David Ford, who participated in the Lambeth Conference of 1998, rightly noted that although "most of us have studied the Bible over many years" and "are aware of various academic approaches to it," we have "also lived in it" and "inhabited it, through worship, preaching, teaching and meditation." As such, Ford observes, "The Bible in the Church is like a city we have lived in for a long time." We may not be able to account for the history of every building or the architecture on every street, but we know our way around and it is a source of life to each of us.[1]

That said, we have not done as much as we should in acquainting the inhabitants of that famed city with the architecture that lies within. So, as risky as it may seem, it is important to set out an introduction to the highlights of that city—which this series proposes to explore at length. Perhaps the best way in which to broach that task is to provide a handful of descriptors.

The first of those descriptors that leaps to mind is familiar, basic, and forever debated: *authoritative*. Years ago I was asked by a colleague who belonged to the Evangelical Free Church why someone with as much obvious interest in the Bible would be an Episcopal priest. I responded, "Because we read the whole of Scripture and not just the parts of it that suit us." Scripture has been and continues to play a singular role in the life of the Anglican Communion, but it has rarely been used in the sharply prescriptive fashion that has characterized some traditions.

Some have characterized this approach as an attempt to navigate a *via media* between overbearing control and an absence of accountability.[2] But I think it is far more helpful to describe the tensions not as a matter of steering a course between two different and competing priorities, but as the complex dance necessary to live under a very different, but typically Anglican notion of authority itself. Authority, you see, shares the same root as the word "to author" and as such, refers first and foremost, not to the *power* to *control* with all that both of those words suggest, but to the capacity to *author creativity*, with all that both of those words suggest. As such, the function of Scripture is to carve out a creative space in which the work of the Holy Spirit can yield the very kind of fruit associated with its work in the Church. The difficulty, of course, is that for that space to be creative, it is also necessary for it to have boundaries, much like the boundaries we establish for other kinds of genuinely creative freedom—the practice of scales for concert pianists, the discipline of work at the bar that frees the ballerina, or the guidance that parents provide for their children. Defined in this way, it is possible to see the boundaries around that creative space as barriers to be eliminated, or as walls that provide protection, but they are neither.

And so the struggle continues with the authority of Scripture. From time to time in the Anglican Communion, it has been and will be treated as the raw material of buttresses that protect us from the complexity of navigating without error the world in which we live. At other times, it will be treated as the ancient remains of a city to be cleared away in favor of a brave new world. But both approaches are rooted, not in the limitations of Scripture, but in our failure to welcome the creative space we have been given.

For that reason, at their best, Anglican approaches to Scripture are also *illuminative*. William Sloan Coffin once observed that the problem with Americans and the Bible is that we read it like a drunk uses a lamppost. We lean on it, we don't use it for illumination. Leaning on Scripture—or having the lamppost taken out completely—are simply two very closely related ways of failing to acknowledge the creative space provided by Scripture. But once the creative space is recognized for what it is, then the importance of reading Scripture illuminatively becomes apparent. Application of the insight Scripture provides into who we are and what we might become is not something that can be prescribed or mapped out in detail. It is only a conversation with Scripture, marked by humility that can begin to spell out the particulars. Reading Scripture is, then, in the Anglican tradition a delicate and demanding task, that involves both the careful listening for the voice of God and courageous conversation with the world around us.

It is, for that reason, an approach that is also marked by *critical engagement* with the text itself. It is no accident that from 1860 to 1900 the three best-known names in the world of biblical scholarship were Anglican priests, two of whom were Bishops: B. F. Westcott, J. B. Lightfoot, and F. J. A. Hort. Together the three made contributions to both the church and the critical study of the biblical text that became a defining characteristic of Anglican life.

Of the three, Westcott's contribution, perhaps, best captures the balance. Not only did his work contribute to a critical text of the Greek Testament that would eventually serve as the basis for the English Revised Version, but as Bishop of Durham he also convened a conference of Christians to discuss the arms race in Europe, founded the Christian Social Union, and mediated the Durham coal strike of 1892.

The English roots of the tradition are not the only, or even the defining characteristic of Anglican approaches to Scripture. The church, no less than the rest of the world, has been forever changed by the process of globalization, which has yielded a rich *diversity* that complements the traditions once identified with the church.

Scripture in Uganda, for example, has been read with an emphasis on private, allegorical, and revivalist applications. The result has been a tradition in large parts of East Africa which stresses the reading of Scripture on one's own; the direct application made to the contemporary situation without reference to the setting of the original text; and the combination of personal testimony with the power of public exhortation.

At the same time, however, globalization has brought that tradition into conversation with people from other parts of the Anglican Communion as the church in Uganda has sought to bring the biblical text to bear on its efforts to address the issues of justice, poverty, war, disease, food shortage, and education. In such a dynamic environment, the only thing that one can say with certainty is that neither the Anglican Communion, nor the churches of East Africa, will ever be the same again.

Authoritative, illuminative, critical, and varied—these are not the labels that one uses to carve out an approach to Scripture that can be predicted with any kind of certainty. Indeed, if the word *dynamic*—just used—is added to the list, perhaps all that one can predict is still more change! And, for that reason, there will be observers who (not without reason) will argue that the single common denominator in this series is that each of the authors also happens to be an Anglican. (There might even be a few who will dispute that!)

But such is the nature of life in any city, including one shaped by the Bible. We influence the shape of its life, but we are also shaped and nurtured by it. And if that city is of God's making, then to force our own design on the streets and buildings around us is to disregard the design that the chief architect has in mind.

—Frederick W. Schmidt
Series Editor

AUTOBIOGRAPHICAL NOTE

Writing this book on the Gospel of John brings together things that are most important to me. In it meet the analytical tools of scholars and faithful, hopeful people wrestling with Scripture in and outside of churches. This conversation like the gospel itself straddles theology and poetry. This meeting happens at a poignant, critical, and liminal time in the church and the world and in some ways in my own life as well.

I have learned from scholars on John and from reading the gospel in church Sunday after Sunday, preaching it and hearing it preached. I have found that not all the time, but much of the time, insights from scholarship enhance understanding and pleasure of reading Scripture and increase its power to convert and to motivate. I have seen over and over again that talking back to a text, asking it questions, and even resisting it does not diminish its sacredness but rather adds to it. The audience for this book combines the two groups of people who have been most valuable to me, seminary students and the people of parishes I have visited and served.

In college I studied English along with religion and part of me still wants to be a professor of poetry or even better, a poet. Writing this book has allowed me to explore how the wonderful narratives in John work as stories, as dramas, and to retell some of them myself. In college I learned to read poetry, novels, and plays with a combination of analytic engagement and detachment. Later at the Harvard Divinity School, Professor George W. MacRae, S.J., introduced me to the Gospel of John and taught me how to attend closely to the text. He defined exegesis as "reading Scripture with maximum attention and curiosity." This marvelous minimalist phrase could also be said to describe the way I learned to read poetry and other literature in college. Developing an awareness of the poetic means by which John conveys its theology deepens our understanding of the message.

I have grown up in a society and a church in conflict over who leads and who follows, who has the authority to interpret and to speak, and how to live together as people of different religious faiths. As a young woman, I was ordained in the Episcopal Church during a period of ferment and renewal. The disputes of that time remain unresolved among peoples of different backgrounds and histories. The issues of vision, voice, and authority are played out in the Gospel of John among the characters Thomas, Mary and Martha, Mary Magdalene, Peter, and the disciple whom Jesus loved. In its vision of the community of friends the gospel offers hope, and in Jesus' promise of the Paraclete it makes room for surprise and ongoing prophesy.

Writing this book has been what scholars may not often admit to—fun. May it be a companion for your reading of John and a provocation to life-giving conversation.

—Cynthia Briggs Kittredge
Austin, Texas
August 1, 2007

INTRODUCTION

An Expansive Reading

For many people today, the Gospel of John is the gospel that separates, excludes, defines, and demands. Jesus' words, "I am the way, the truth, and the life, no one comes to the Father except through me," claim that Jesus Christ is the exclusive way to salvation. The quotation of John 3:16, "God so loved the world," has become a kind of slogan for Christian truth claims in public sports arenas. Over the course of history, influenced by its hair-raising rhetoric of hostility toward Jesus' Jewish opponents, Christians have indeed separated from, excluded, and judged their Jewish neighbors.

However, as I have taught John in parish halls and seminary classrooms and preached from it in worship over the past twenty years, I have come to appreciate the gospel in a very different way. I see it now as the gospel that crosses over and includes. Yes, it is indeed demanding, but it is patient and generous in its repeated invitations to see and believe. Line after line, page after page, sign after sign, the Gospel of John demonstrates its generosity. As the Samaritan woman violates rules in her conversation with Jesus at the well and as the risen Jesus ignores the closed doors to the room where the fearful disciples are huddled, so the gospel itself breaks boundaries, opens doors, and displays a vision of a colorful, diverse, even ecstatic community of friends of Jesus.

Yes, it is indeed demanding, but it is patient and generous in its repeated invitations to see and believe. Line after line, page after page, sign after sign, the gospel of John demonstrates its generosity.

I still struggle with how to teach and preach the language of hatred also prominent in the gospel and how to take seriously the potential for violence the language can provoke. But I see the complexity of John's story of Jesus in a richer way, as I have read the whole of the book with its strange twists and turns, abrupt transitions, and overlooked episodes. Beyond the headlines and in the long haul of the gospel—in people's extended conversations with Jesus, in the long sequence of signs of Jesus' glory, in his conversation with God in prayer, and the visits with his friends at Easter, I see clues to a vision of open community. The vision pushes beyond even some the boundaries very soon to be set up and reinforced by the church and presses against the limits on ecstatic vision and prophecy that some Christian leaders recommend. The vision is at some points in tension with the emphasis of other authors in the New Testament who claim, for example, that a specific body of teaching is authoritative for the church or that the twelve apostles and their descendents are its only legitimate leaders. If readers become alert to and follow these clues, they come to see what I call an "expansive" reading of John. Ancient readers read John in different ways, some emphasizing the parts which closed off and defined and some the parts that opened up and defied. In the chapters that follow, I will attend to these clues and explore them, and I will share my conviction that reading John in this way offers treasures to our embattled world and divided churches. To use the gospel's own language, it offers abundant life.

In the following pages I will explore these clues toward an expansive reading:

- God commits God-self to the world and all its creatures and comes to dwell.
- Jesus makes himself known through visible, material signs.
- Jesus creates a community of beloved friends whose leaders are those who have leaned on his bosom, conversed and argued with him, and who listen to the Spirit.
- Jesus tries over and over again in creative and diverse ways to show his glory and give life.

We will open our conversation in chapter 1 by talking about John's relationship with the three other gospels in the New Testament, about how to think about its author, and about how the gospel understands and conveys the history of Jesus. Chapter 2 will focus on the first clue, God's commitment to creation through the Logos, by exploring the unique feature of John, the poetic prologue in John 1:1–18. Chapter 3 will follow the second clue, Jesus' self-revelation, and attend to the character and purpose of the signs in John, particularly Jesus' generous provision of wine at the wedding at Cana and his feeding the multitude in the wilderness. In chapter 4 I will wrestle with

Logos: the divine wisdom manifest in the creation, government, and redemption of the world and often identified with the second person of the Trinity

the most difficult challenge to an expansive reading of John—the negative portrait of the Jews and the language of hate and opposition of the world and God. Here the focus will be the story of the bereaved family and their grieving Jewish friends at Bethany and the encounter of Jesus with the woman of Samaria. Chapter 5 investigates the third clue, the community Jesus creates, by rereading the story of the foot washing supper, Mary of Bethany's anointing of Jesus, the role of the beloved disciple, and the presence of the spirit which this gospel calls the Paraclete. Chapter 6 focuses on the last of the clues and emphasizes

Paraclete: literally, advocate, intercessor, from *parakalein* to invoke, from *para-* + *kalein* to call

how many times and in how many different ways this gospel works upon the reader. Here we will analyze the series of Easter stories which conclude the gospel.

An Anglican Reading

I share insights drawn from my conversation with John in teaching and preaching in order that you might have conversations with this gospel in your own neighborhoods and parishes. Conversation with Scripture requires curiosity and close attention. It asks for willingness to appreciate and courage to challenge. Such conversation is informed by knowledge of the history and culture at the time the text was written, of its particular literary features, and of how the text has been interpreted in different periods of the church's life. The Anglican scholarly tradition has encouraged the exercise of these skills in the study of Scripture. As a priest and scholar of the Episcopal Church, I have been influenced by the values of reason and free inquiry that have shaped the academic field of biblical studies. I share with other scholars engaged in work of justice the conviction that interpreting the Scripture of our tradition transforms us and the world we serve. And at the same time I have pursued this study, taught and preached the gospel, within the broad embrace of the sacramental life of the church. This combination of freedom, conviction, and faith has characterized my approach to the Bible as an Episcopalian.

So this reading is Anglican on one level, simply because the guide to this particular conversation about John is an Anglican. As I reflect on the results of this reading, I see another feature that points to an Anglican approach to Scripture. This reading emphasizes Christ's kinship with creation and veers away from the tendency to sectarianism of the high priestly prayer (John 17:12–17). It tries to view John's unique contribution to the canon without collapsing or harmonizing it into an artificial unity. The qualities of mediation and discernment are prized by a good part of the Anglican tradition. The writers of John in their own culture and historical period were certainly not Anglican, but rather more intense, more potentially sectarian, more radical than what we think of as English or American Anglican. I have tried to draw attention to some of the wonderfully radical features of this gospel which may have become obscured by being overly familiar. I think that somehow saturation in the Anglican ethos allows me, like other Anglican scholars, to see and appreciate tensions within a text, cope with ambiguity, and handle it gently. Our inquiring and analyzing and even playing with interpretations of sacred texts is all done in trust in the Spirit and in the comprehensive strength of our common worship, and all is pursued with confidence in the ongoing activity of the other Advocate whom Jesus sent and who lives among us.

Many Anglicans know their Bible mediated through the prayer book liturgy. Images and words from the Fourth Gospel shine through the prayer book services. Throughout this book I will quote Johannine motifs from hymns and prayers, in hope that this conversation with John will strengthen and amplify these echoes of Scripture in the Book of Common Prayer.

The Gospel of John is an exceptionally, almost infinitely rich text, which invites conversation. My own conversations have been tutored by wise scholars whose own faith traditions are Roman Catholic, Protestant, and Jewish. The names of some of them appear in the bibliographical section at the end of each chapter. Of course I would like this expansive reading to be persuasive, but even more I would like it to encourage your own reading and wrestling with this gospel.

CHAPTER ONE

John Among the Gospels: Orienting John in History and Canon

The most important questions to explore at the outset of our conversation are how to conceive the relationship of John with the other gospels, how to understand the author of John, and how to imagine that the gospel tells the history of Jesus. These are immensely complex scholarly issues, but for the sake of this exploration I will try to simplify them and share how I have found it helpful to think about these questions. An expansive reading of John appreciates the distinctiveness of John's theological and artistic perspective, and views the difference from the gospels of Matthew, Mark, and Luke as positive, creative tension. It understands the author of John, not as a named apostle, but as a leader or leaders of a community, drawing on the tradition of the disciple whom Jesus loved but does not name, who tell the story of Jesus and of themselves. Finally it conceives of the history reported by the gospel to be the story of Jesus told and retold by a community who elabo-

> An expansive reading of John appreciates the distinctiveness of John's theological and artistic perspective, and views the difference from the gospels of Matthew, Mark, and Luke as positive, creative tension.

rates upon that history as time passes and who rethink and retell Jesus' words and deeds in light of their sense of his ongoing presence with them.

Not the "Fifth Wheel" But the Fourth Gospel

Matthew, Mark, Luke, and John,
Bless the bed that I lie on.
Four corners to my bed,
Four angels round my head;
One to watch, and one to pray,
And two to bear my soul away.

Bible readers know John as one of four gospels in the New Testament. We begin with this fact because the existence of the other gospels, Matthew, Mark, and Luke, affects how modern readers understand John. We know that there are several accounts of Jesus' life, of which John is one. This reality is summarized in the title for the Gospel of John, "The Fourth Gospel." To unpack this obvious fact, we need to review how the gospels came to be written, got their names, and became part of an authoritative collection of Scripture, or canon. This review will introduce how we will read John in relationship with the three other canonical gospels.

Canonization of the Four Gospels

The gospels that came to be known as Matthew, Mark, Luke, and John were composed by anonymous authors from traditions about Jesus in the decades following his death and resurrection. These gospels were among various kinds of writings, especially letters of Paul, which were acquiring authority for Christian communities gathered for Scripture study, prayer, and worship. When the gospels were first written, those who used them considered them sacred writings, but they were not "in a Bible" as we know it. The "Scripture" read by believers in Jesus was the Hebrew Bible in its Greek form, the Septuagint. That canon of Scripture was also not fixed, but became settled as rabbinic Judaism organized itself in the late first and second centuries of the common era. At the time they were written, the gospels did not name their authors, but in the second and third centuries the Christian writers known as the Church Fathers, or the patristic writers, discussed these books, attributed them to apostles in the time of Jesus, and explained traditions about their apostolic origins. At the same time they spoke about which books were considered to have authority and which books were questioned and why. Naming the authors of the gospels was part of the process we now call "canonization" which happened gradually between the second and fourth centuries. Canonization was a key part of the process of describing Christian orthodoxy which at this time was taking shape and becoming specifically defined.

Patristic: of or relating to the fathers of the early Christian church or their writings

In the first half of the second century (100–150 CE) from what we know, it appears that the Gospel of John was valued not so much among those writers who shaped orthodoxy, but by those Christians whom the orthodox writers later strongly opposed, the Valentinian Christians. The first commentary on John was written by Heracleon (160–180) and there is no other reference to the apostle John or to the gospel in the early first century.[3] The popularity of John among these other Christian groups may have cast suspicion upon this gospel on the part of some writers. By the time of the formation of the canon, John was embraced and claimed by orthodox Christianity.

Canonize: to include in the biblical canon

The changes in the ancient reputation of John gives rise to the question of John's relationship with what scholars used to call "Gnosticism," or to other gospels which did not become part of the canon, such as the Gospel of Thomas or the Gospel of Mary Magdalene. This question is important because of the extraordinary popular attention that these noncanonical gospels have received, especially since the book and the movie of *The Da Vinci Code*. Some scholars argue that John was written to oppose the approach to Christianity of the Gospel of Thomas.[4] Others have claimed that John has characteristics typical of these heterodox groups. I have found that the strict opposition between "Gnosticism" and "orthodoxy" interferes with a sensitive and appreciative reading of John's gospel. The complex fabric of John resists simple categorization. I will point out where John's perspective is not in strict harmony with the perspective of develop-

Orthodoxy: an orthodox (established, approved, or conventional) belief, doctrine, custom, etc.

ing orthodoxy, such as in its view of leadership in the community and the role of ongoing vision and prophecy. An expansive reading attempts to move beyond the either-or question of "Gnostic or not?" in order to encourage both understanding and questioning of the vision of this gospel.

Patristic Interpretation of John within the Four Gospel Canon

As the four gospel canon came into being, the church fathers grappled with how the gospel fit or did not fit with the stories of Jesus told in the three gospels that had become important in the church. These leaders asked what seminarians and college students and parish readers continue to ask: "Is it OK that there is more than one version of the story of Jesus in the Bible? Does a variety of versions somehow undermine their claim to truth?" Marcion, a popular church leader, used one gospel, a version of Luke, and a number of letters of Paul. The second century ascetic Tatian and those who followed him used a harmony of the gospels called *Diatesseron*. Scholars know some facts about canonization from lists of canonical books and comments in the writings of the church fathers, but they are not able to reconstruct exactly how the canon came into being. History kept no schedule of meetings, recorded no minutes, nor spelled out the process in detail. In fact it is unlikely that these decisions were made in meetings; it is most likely that certain writings gained their authority by their circulation and use by Christian communities. But we do know that the answer on which orthodoxy came to agree was "Yes, it's OK. There must be more than one, and there cannot be more than four." The classic explanation of this fact of four gospels is made by Irenaeus in the second century:

> The Gospels could not possibly be either more or less in number than they are. Since there are four zones of the world in which we live, and four principal winds, the church . . . fittingly has four pillars, breathing out incorruption and revivifying men. From this it is clear that the Logos, the artificer of all things, he who sits upon the cherubim and

sustains all things . . . gave us the gospel in four-fold form, but held together by one spirit . . . For the cherubim have four faces . . . [and] the Gospels, in which Christ is enthroned, are like these. Adv. Haer. XI, 8.[5]

Irenaeus knew that four gospels had achieved prominence in the church, and he makes their number a virtue rather than a liability. The confidence and solidity implied by Irenaeus is echoed in the children's nursery prayer. Just as there are four posts on a bed, there are four gospels, like angels surrounding a child's body, each with a particular job.

The four gospel canon came to be the solution to the problem of more than one gospel in the early church, but it raised particular questions about John. Of the four gospels, three, Matthew, Mark, and Luke, tell the story of Jesus in roughly similar order and resemble each other closely. Modern scholars use the term "synoptic" for Matthew, Mark, and Luke. John, however, uses a distinctive language, contains different stories and characters, and has some other important divergences. For example, John places Jesus' visit to the temple early in the gospel rather than before his entry into Jerusalem as in Matthew, Mark, and Luke. In the Fourth Gospel, during his final meal with the disciples, Jesus does not speak of the bread and wine as his body and blood, but washes the disciples' feet, teaches its meaning, and commands them to do the same. When they commented on the gospels, the church fathers noticed that John fit awkwardly with the others. On first glance, John was the "black sheep" of the gospels, and the church fathers had to explain how it properly belonged among the gospels. However, as the reputation of John grew and it became a valued source for doctrine in later church writings, the misfit gospel became the one which encompassed all. As a result the three synoptic gospels came to be read in light of doctrines based on language in John. For example, Irenaeus uses the title the *Logos*, a term from John, to describe the creator of the four-fold gospel canon. So, the gospel which could have been the hardest to assimi-

Synoptic: 1. taking the same point of view; 2. relating to or being the first three gospels of the New Testament, which share content, style, and order of events and which differ largely from John

However, as the reputation of John grew and it became a valued source for doctrine in later church writings, the misfit gospel became the one which encompassed all.

5

late with the others became the last, the Fourth, the one which completes Irenaeus' unity of four.

John in Its Own Words

In this conversation with John we will read it neither as the misfit gospel nor as the one which explains all the others. Rather, as much as possible, we will take our cues from the gospel's own understanding of itself, and try to figure out how it expresses the significance of Jesus and the story of his life and death. The writer or writers of John did not know it would be part of a four gospel canon, although they did know the existence of many traditions about Jesus' "signs" and even perhaps many books. To harmonize John with the others—to make it logically consistent—is to lose the distinctive insights that this gospel can teach. For example, the opening poem in John's prologue is not a Christmas story like the nativity narratives in Matthew and Luke. Likewise, to say that John assumes that Jesus instituted the Eucharist at the last supper is to miss the gravity of the foot-washing as the "sacramental" act of the dinner. As we get to know John's outlook and literary style well, we will learn to hear "in stereo" and at times make comparison with a version of the same incident in Matthew, Mark, or Luke. We will begin to see how John interprets Jesus' traditions and expresses them in a unique Johannine mode, as though using a different dialect or another key to explore the meaning of Jesus.

Although it is tempting to interpret John with the categories of the fully defined orthodoxy of the Nicene Creed, we will stay with the language of the gospel itself and seek to understand Jesus in the categories of the author or authors of John. For example, John's gospel was a prime source upon which the church fathers reflected when developing the doctrine of the Trinity, but we do not find the Trinity as a theological category in this gospel. Although orthodox Christology came to be articulated in the creeds, that Jesus was "fully God and fully human," what we find in John is the Logos poem that opens the gospel followed by stories of Jesus who speaks and acts in ways that cannot be easily categorized as "divine" or "human." The gospel cites and encompasses many titles for Jesus and includes statements about Jesus' equality with God juxtaposed with statements of his subordination to God. Getting to know this rich gospel in its particularity enables us to hear its theological voice and allows the gospel to work upon us.

John's own description of its purpose is critically important to interpreting this gospel. The writing of the signs is designed to evoke belief, conversion, and transformation of those who read. The Fourth Gospel states its purpose:

> Now Jesus did many other signs in the presence of his disciples, which are not written in this book. But these are written so that you may come to believe [continue to believe] that Jesus is the Messiah, the Son of God, and that through believing you may have life in his name. (John 20:30–31)[6]

These verses tell the reader explicitly why the gospel is being written. The narrator directly addresses the reader as "you" and states that these signs are written "so that you may come to believe that Jesus is the Messiah, the Son of God." This gospel expresses self-consciousness about its "written-ness." Some manuscripts have the present tense of "believe" and others have the aorist tense, a form of the past tense in Greek. If one takes the verb as aorist, the verse implies that the purpose of the gospel is to elicit belief that does not yet exist. If one chooses the present tense, the option that the NRSV includes in the textual notes (continue to believe), then the purpose of the gospel is to strengthen the faith of those who already believe. In John to believe is to embrace God's revelation in Christ.[7] Believing is both relational and cognitive. The faith that the gospel intends to elicit or to strengthen also has a purpose, so that "you may have life in his name." This giving of "life" is the way this gospel speaks of salvation, the benefit of faith.

A second distinctive feature of this gospel is its ending. In teaching the gospels, I always ask students to look with extra care at the beginning and ending of each gospel, and sometimes I suggest beginning at the end. John is unusual in that it appears to have two endings. The summary of the purpose of the gospel looks to be a kind of conclusion, because it sounds like a very fitting ending. But immediately after this conclusion, the gospel resumes with another episode beginning with the unspecific phrase "after these things."

This episode tells of another appearance of Jesus to his followers after his death. It is almost as though a writer took the first conclusion (20:30–31) seriously and included another story about a sign Jesus did in the presence of his disciples. The first "ending" appears to be ignored as an ending, but what it affirms is not eliminated.

The additional episode tells of a fishing trip with some disciples and a breakfast on the beach with Jesus. After this story, the gospel ends again with these words: "This is the disciple who is testifying to these things and has written them, and we know that his testimony is true. But there are also many other things that Jesus did; if every one of them were written down, I suppose that the world itself could not contain the books that would be written" (John 21:24–25).

With the statement which begins, "this is the disciple," the narrator draws attention to the authoritative source for "these things." The disciple is the "disciple whom Jesus loved" who is mentioned in the previous verse. This character has been called attention to once before, in John 19:35, at the time when blood and water came from Jesus' side: "(He who saw this has testified so that you also may believe. His testimony is true, and he knows that he tells the truth.)" (John 19:35).

In the ending verses the author claims connection between the disciple whom Jesus loved and the testimony, writing, and truth of this book. The character does not name himself nor is the person named by the narrator. The verse does not say, "I, John, have written them" or, "the disciple, John, has written them."

This ending, like the first, acknowledges that there are many other things that Jesus did. It may be significant that unlike the first statement it does not call them signs or mention the presence of the disciples. The narrator speculates that the number of books filled with these signs could not be contained by the world—they are infinite. This ending admits that books cannot contain all the things that Jesus did, and by doing so ends, instead of with conclusiveness, on a surprising note of openness.

One can think of this unusual feature of the Gospel of John in a number of ways—the gospel has two endings, a double ending, an ending which isn't an ending, or no ending. And at the end the text refers enigmatically to the individual who testifies to the truth of the things written. These observations call for interpretation and lead to the questions of authorship and to historicity to which we now turn.

The Author of John

The ancient traditions about the author and date of the Gospel of John give information about the process of canonization and what the church fathers thought was important to explain about the origins of the gospel. For them it was necessary to assert that an apostle of Jesus wrote the gospel and to give an account of how it diverged from the other three gospels. Irenaeus writes: "Finally John, the disciple of the Lord, who had also lain on his breast, himself published the gospel, while he was residing at Ephesus in Asia."[8] Tradition attributed this gospel to John, the son of Zebedee, the disciple described in the synoptic gospels as one called by Jesus with his brother from his nets. Gradually the name of the apostle John, John the son of Zebedee, and the beloved disciple came to be identified.

For the patristic writers, apostolic authorship and authority were closely identified. Modern biblical scholars, on the other hand, are most interested in determining a likely author and date for the gospel which best explains the variety of references to the gospel in the church fathers and makes sense of the language and concepts of the gospel. They conclude that the evidence weighs heavily against the identification of the John of Zebedee with the beloved disciple or the author of the gospel. They agree with the patristic writers that it is the last of the four gospels to be written. They date the gospel near the end of the first century, around 90 to 100 CE. They think that it may have originated in Ephesus in Asia Minor or in Antioch in Syria.

When we look closely at the gospel's statement of its purpose, its claim to be linked to the tradition about Jesus seen by the beloved disciple, and its first and second concluding statements, we can explain these features of the text by imagining that the gospel was written and edited over a period of time. During that time, for example, the final scene is added as a kind of epilogue to the previous edition of the gospel. If this is so, then the author of John is not a

If this is so, then the author of John is not a single individual, but members of a community over a period of time, who held this gospel dear and adapted it and added to it as time passed.

single individual, but members of a community over a period of time, who held this gospel dear and adapted it and added to it as time passed.

To think of the gospel as being composed over a period of time helps to make sense of the two endings and some of the other inconsistencies in the text. The language of bread and wine in the sermon in John 6 shifts to the terminology of eating flesh and drinking blood. At the end of chapter 14, Jesus appears to complete his address with the instructions, "Rise, let us be on our way" (John 14:31). However, the discourse immediately resumes in the next verses. Such breaks in the smooth telling of the story can be attributed to the "composition history" of the text.

Scholars since Rudolf Bultmann have formulated specific theories about the different stages of editing that the gospel underwent. The most useful and well-known are those of Louis Martyn and Raymond Brown.[9] These scholars associate editorial additions and changes to changing circumstances in the life of this "Johannine" community. They understand that as this community tells the story of Jesus, it also tells its own story of separation and alienation from its neighbors. They explain a significant editorial change, such as the addition of the epilogue, to reflect changed perspectives on the authority of Peter in the Christian community. One can use various images to picture the process of composition of the gospel. One is of a document having been, in either an ancient or modern form, cut and pasted, leaving the editorial seams visible. Another image is of an old tapestry, rewoven, mended, and expanded over the years of its use. Another, highly anachronistic and climactically inappropriate, is of a snowball which collects stones and bits of dirt and grass, along with pieces of ice, as it is rolled and grows to its finished size and position in the completed structure. Whatever image is used to convey this process, it should express the sense of preservation and innovation through faithful use.

A compelling reason for thinking that the gospel underwent rewriting during the history of the community is its confidence in the activity of the Spirit (14:15–17; 15:26; 16:7–8). When Jesus is bidding farewell to the gathered friends, he promises that after he is gone he will ask the Father to send "another *paracletos*" to be with them, here called the "spirit of truth." This term can mean counselor, advocate, the one who testifies or advocates for. It is John's term for the Holy Spirit but it has particular connotations of arguing on behalf of and teaching. Other aspects of the gospel show that the community had a vivid sense of the spirit among them: its emphasis on vision and prophecy and on the infinite number of Jesus' signs. This spirit continued to speak and teach in the community after the exaltation of Jesus' death.[10] With a sense of the presence of the spirit and of the risen Christ among them, it would make sense that the traditions about Jesus would expand, develop, and change. In the life of the community the Paraclete played a role parallel to that of the gospel—evoking belief. Thus in some ways, the Paraclete participates in authorizing this gospel.

The impulse of the church fathers was to link the beloved disciple with a specific name of a disciple of Jesus, because of how important they understood apostolic authorship to be. However, if we are to read John on its own terms, it is more faithful to the spirit of this gospel to allow the beloved disciple, the source for the tradition of Jesus' ministry, to remain unnamed.

John as History

Readers of John, since the time of the church fathers and continuing into modern scholarship, have been perplexed by the question of whether John reflects an accurate history of Jesus. Especially because of the agreement of the three synoptic gospels against the testimony of the Fourth Gospel on some matters, such as the last supper being a Passover meal, for example, some have argued that John is not historically reliable. Other scholars argue that in some features, such as the reason for Jesus' crucifixion being fear for the temple and the nation (John 11:48–50), the details in John are more historically plausible than the other gospels. To answer this question, it is important to notice that the "problem of historical Jesus" was not a "problem" for this gospel. Rather, this gospel claims authoritative connection with an eyewitness (19:35) who testifies truly and has written the things that Jesus did. The truth of the story is based on the reliability of this person. The truth of the story is not focused on accuracy and completeness of research as in the opening of Luke's

Like the other gospels in the canon, the gospel of John is interpreted, symbolically reflected history, and history with life-giving consequences.

gospel, but on the closeness of this disciple to Jesus, exemplified in the posture of reclining next to his bosom, and his or her own faith. It intends to provoke belief in Jesus in the present, by telling the story of the past. Like the other gospels in the canon, the Gospel of John is interpreted, symbolically reflected history, and history with life-giving consequences.

The gospel tells the story of Jesus with the vivid sense that the Paraclete abides with them and continues to remind them and teach them what Jesus said. There is strong evidence that ongoing vision and prophesy was alive in this community. Jesus invites the disciples to "come and see" (1:39) and tells Nathaniel: "Very truly, I tell you. You will see heaven opened and the angels of God ascending and descending upon the Son of Man" (1:51). When the beloved disciple reaches the tomb and goes in, "he saw and believed" (20:8). Mary announces to the disciples "I have seen the Lord" (20:18). Those who cherished Jesus' words and experienced them as giving life did not have the same idea as we do that Jesus said certain things and the words stayed the same forever. Jesus speaks in a different style in John than he does in the synoptics—he talks more about himself than about the kingdom of God. While his words at the last supper are brief in the synoptics, in John Jesus gives a last will and testament covering five chapters (13–17). It is likely that these discourses developed through the reflection on the meaning of Jesus' death and resurrection in the community. The Gospel of John, with its stops and starts and strange turns and resumptions, shows that the story of Jesus for this community is a living story, a story infused with the spirit of the living Jesus.

The gospel of John, with its stops and starts and strange turns and resumptions, shows that the story of Jesus for this community is a living story, a story infused with the spirit of the living Jesus.

A particular community valued the traditions linked to the testimony of this unnamed disciple whom Jesus loved. They told and retold the story in worship as they read Scripture and as they practiced it through baptism, Eucharist, and foot-washing. As they told the story of Jesus, they told the story of their own experience as a community. The story bears marks of that community's history, especially its experience of separation from its origins in the Jewish community. At the same time the gospel tells a cosmic story in which

Jesus descends to the world as revealer. In the world he is rejected by most and is accepted by a few. He is lifted up on the cross and exalted to heaven. Those who have accepted him become his beloved community of friends on earth whom he abides with through the Spirit. These three stories, the story of Jesus, of the community, and of God and the world are intricately interwoven in the narrative of John. So the history in John is always multi-layered history, in which the "history" of Jesus cannot simply be extracted.

The Spiritual Gospel

The question of John's relationship with the other three gospels, its author, and its way of writing history orient us for beginning to read John. These questions coincide in a quotation from Clement of Alexandria which has become one classic way to understand the relationship between John and the synoptic gospels: "Last of all, aware that the physical facts had been recorded in the gospels, encouraged by his pupils and irresistibly moved by the Spirit, John wrote a spiritual gospel."[11]

Clement draws a picture of the apostle, John, who knows the other gospels and who decides to write another. He is not independent, but he relies on disciples and the Holy Spirit. Clement distinguishes between "physical" and "spiritual." He resolves the problem of the divergences between John and the synoptic gospels by calling the three physical and John spiritual. It may be that in this way Clement also resolved the question of historicity—Matthew, Mark, and Luke were grounded in the physical reality of Jesus' history but John was interested in something else—the "spiritual." Many people in churches today hold to some version of this understanding of John as the spiritual gospel.

I have suggested that we read John in its own words and think of its author as a community or sequence of spirit-inspired writers. Its history is a symbolically interpreted, life-giving, and multi-layered story. This approach is obviously not the same as Clement's. However, Clement's understanding sets us a challenge—how to articulate how we understand that John is the "spiritual" gospel. Will we find, like Clement, that physical and spiritual are opposed? What is "spiritual" in Johannine words?

The variation on the story of the Jesus in John need not be a stumbling block to us as we explore what distinctive insights this gospel offers. Unique among the gospels is the way John acknowledges the existence of other traditions of Jesus' deeds and signs and even admits the infinitude of potential books about them. Highly unusual is the way it ends twice and then doesn't really end. This story does not hide, but retains the marks and traces, seams, scars, and shadows, of its past versions. Its principal characters, Nicodemus, the woman of Samaria, the chronically sick man at the pool, the man born blind, Mary, Martha, Lazarus of Bethany, and Thomas, are unknown to the other gospels and do not substitute for the twelve named disciples so important to Mark, Matthew, and Luke. Among the friends, chief apostles are Martha and Mary Magdalene who perform authoritative roles in John. One of its heroes has no name. These unusual features suggest that this gospel is potentially the most expansive of the four gospels, the gospel that works against the orthodox impulse for finishing and closing. The four gospel canon says that it is right that there is more than one version of the story of Jesus, and the Gospel of John implies that there are even more. One way to think of John is as the fourth post of the four-poster bed providing comforting solidity and permanence in conjunction with the others. Or alternatively, as we explore its details, we might think of John acting among the gospels as the leavening agent, keeping the canon bubbling and full of air, or as the breath keeping the body alive, or as the door open to other worlds.

Continuing the Conversation . . .

Commentaries and studies which are useful introductions to John's gospel are, Raymond Brown, *The Gospel According to John, Anchor Bible Commentary* (New York: Doubleday, 1966–70); Raymond Brown, *The Community of the Beloved Disciple* (New York: Paulist Press, 1979); R. Alan. Culpepper, *The Gospel and Letters of John, Interpreting Biblical Texts* (Nashville: Abingdon, 1998); Sandra M. Schneiders, *Written that you May Believe: Encountering Jesus in the Fourth Gospel* (New York: Crossroad, 1999, 2003); D. Moody Smith, *The Theology of the Gospel of John, New Testament Theology* (Cambridge: Cambridge University Press, 1995).

On the issue of historicity and the relationship of John with the synoptic gospels, see J. Louis Martyn, *History and Theology in the Fourth Gospel* (1st ed.) (New York: Harper & Row, 1968). D. Moody Smith, *John Among the Gospels: The Relationship in Twentieth-Century Research* (Minneapolis: Fortress Press, 1992).

The Prologue of John

In the beginning was the Word,
and the Word was with God,
and the Word was God.
[2] He was in the beginning with God.

[3] All things came into being through him,
and without him not one thing came into being.
What has come into being [4] in him was life,
and the life was the light of all people.
[5] The light shines in the darkness,
and the darkness did not overcome it.

[6] *There was a man sent from God, whose name was John.* [7] *He came as a witness to testify to the light, so that all might believe through him.* [8] *He himself was not the light, but he came to testify to the light.* [9] *The true light, which enlightens everyone, was coming into the world.*

[10] He was in the world,
and the world came into being through him;
yet the world did not know him.
[11] He came to what was his own,
and his own people did not accept him.
[12] But to all who received him, who believed in his name,
he gave power to become children of God,

[13] *who were born, not of blood or of the will of the flesh or of the will of man, but of God.*

[14] And the Word became flesh
and lived among us,
and we have seen his glory,
the glory as of a father's only son,
full of grace and truth.

15 *(John testified to him and cried out, "This was he of whom I said, 'He who comes after me ranks ahead of me because he was before me.'")*

16 From his fullness we have all received,
grace upon grace.

17 *The law indeed was given through Moses; grace and truth came through Jesus Christ.*

18 No one has ever seen God.
It is God the only Son,
who is close to the Father's heart,
who has made him known.

CHAPTER TWO

Beginning at the Beginning: The Gospel Prologue

We give thanks to you, O God, for the goodness and love which you have made known to us in creation; in the calling of Israel to be your people; in your Word spoken through the prophets; and above all in the Word made flesh, Jesus, your Son.

EUCHARISTIC PRAYER B,
BOOK OF COMMON PRAYER, PAGE 368

The Gospel of John begins with a hymn which tells the whole story of the gospel in a succinct and poetic form. The hymn employs its own distinctive vocabulary of "light," "life," and "world," and is patterned with regular rhythm and solemn cadence. The main character of the story is the *Logos*, a word which means "word" or "speech" and has wide literary, religious, and philosophic resonances. Only in this passage of John does this word for Jesus occur.

Probably the most well-known of all passages from Scripture, these verses, commonly known as the prologue, at one time were publicly recited at the end of the Eucharist and referred to as the "last gospel." Scholars agree that this passage is the hermeneutical, or interpretive, key to the gospel. Rudolf Bultmann used the metaphor of a musical overture of the gospel in which melodies are introduced at the opening to be elaborated upon in the rest of the sym-

Hermeneutics: the theory and methodology of interpretation, especially of scriptural text

phony.[12] Literary critic Alan Culpepper speaks of the prologue as a lens through which the gospel should be viewed.[13]

In this chapter we will focus on certain features of the prologue and explore their significance for reading the whole gospel. First, we will explore why it is significant to begin the gospel with a hymn. We will attend to the shape of the hymn, its structure and movement, and the signs of its history of composition. We will ask about the meaning of the term *Word*, or *Logos*, and inquire into its ancestors in Jewish thought. We will describe the story of the troubled visit of the Logos to the world, and the life-giving choice offered to those who believe. Finally we will integrate the theme of the creation of all things in the prologue with the motifs of creation in the narrative. An expansive reading of John emphasizes God's commitment to creation by way of the *Logos*, through whom God creates all things and with whom God comes to dwell.

Looking at the Hymn

The introduction to the gospel is in the form of a hymn, a song sung by the faithful in praise of the Logos, a word this poem uses for Christ. Like many of the other Christological hymns in the New Testament (Phil 2:6–11, Heb 1:2–4, Col 1:15–20), this hymn speaks of Jesus as existing from the beginning and participating in creation, descending to earth, and being exalted by God. All these hymns use language of wisdom mythology to describe Jesus, dwelling with God, coming to find a home among humans, and returning to God. Hymns are by definition corporate, sung by a community, and doxological, giving thanks to God. Scholars have proposed many theories about who the original author of the hymn was, whether the hymn came from somewhere else for a different purpose, and how and why it was adapted to speak of Christ for this community and this gospel. However, what is important here is that the gospel begins with a communal song, a poem rather than an identification of the author, an explanation of his or her credentials, or an episode in Jesus' life. Attention to the poem's theological content should not obscure the liturgical and celebratory character of this beginning.

The prologue is called a hymn because of its form in stanzas and its parallel structure. Even in English, the rhythmic quality of the passage can be clearly heard. In the text of the poem printed at the opening of this chapter, I have showed the stanzaic divisions in the layout of the text. When you read the passage, you will also hear portions which seem to interrupt the lyrics of the hymn with commentary or argument. I have indicated those lines by printing them as prose and putting them in italics. Not every scholar reconstructs the hymn and its interruptions in exactly the same way, but this layout represents a general consensus.[14]

These prose interruptions in verses 6–9, 13, 15, and 17 appear to be commenting upon the poem, at times amplifying or clarifying it. The first and second pertain to John, a historical person and the only proper name in the poem until Jesus Christ in verse 17. The last speaks of Moses and the law and compares its gifts with the gifts of Jesus Christ. While the poetic sections have a solemn, declarative tone, confident and secure, the prose commentary sounds more argumentative, a bit quarrelsome, and addresses what appear to be more technical issues, i.e., how exactly were God's children begotten? Such close observation of the text indicates that over the course of its use, this part of the text underwent editing or change; these different tones represent "layers" in the history of composition. Raymond Brown attributes these layers to "successive editing in Johannine circles" indicating that the various writers/editors generally agreed but made corrections or changes as time passed. These are the traces of the text's history we discussed in chapter 1. As you begin to hear shifts in tone in the prologue and throughout the text of John, you can start to listen for tension within the theological perspectives of the text—to understand how the text represents a conversation in a community over a period of time and how it can provoke a conversation among its readers.

Chiasm: a figure of speech by which the order of words in the first of two parallel clauses is reversed in the second

As with all literature, the shape of the hymn reflects its meaning—here the poetic story moves from descent to ascent, from past to present, and from distant to intimate. It is structured as a chiasm in which the emphatic verse, the turning point in the structure, is verse 12: "But to all who received him, who believed in his name, he gave power to become children of God."

The plot of the story begins with creation John 1:1–5. The next major development in the plot is told in verses 10 and 11 in which the Word is not accepted by "his own." This rejection is a tragic irony which later episodes of the gospel will illustrate. The turning point, verse 12, contrasts the rejection of the Word with the assertion that the Word gives power to those who do accept to become children of God. The next episode describes the coming of the Word to the world as becoming flesh and affirms that "we have seen his glory" (1:14). The final verses celebrate this vision and its gifts: fullness, love, grace, and truth (1:16–18). Verses 14 and 18 introduce a new term, "Son," who has made God known. The poem tells the story from a long-distance perspective and employs abstract language of word and God, light and darkness. The prose additions use proper names of John and Moses, but those names too are placed in the overall cosmic perspective of the hymn. The "author" of the poem is understated or submerged—only appearing in the first person plural "we" in verses 14 and 16. This "we" speaks with authority and possesses an omniscient perspective on creation and the coming of the *Logos*.

Other Gospel Beginnings

Comparing the prologue of John with the openings of the other gospels sets John's distinct perspective into high relief. Matthew lists the ancestors of Jesus in a genealogy then tells of the angelic announcement to Joseph of the meaning and import of Mary's pregnancy. After an author's dedication, Luke begins with the parents of John, his conception and birth, and a detailed scene of Jesus' birth in a stable, the picture we think of as a "nativity scene." Both these beginnings are "close up" views of Jesus' birth in history with the names of his parents and relatives, and both interpret the significance of Jesus through details in the angelic announcement: for Matthew "God with us," and for Luke "a Savior, Christ the Lord." The opening verses of John do not use the name of Jesus or his parents. The only proper name which appears in the opening of the prologue is the name of John, who appears as a kind of human interruption in the cosmic scheme. In contrast to the more mundane and homely details of Matthew and Luke's nativity, John is highly abstract and distant. Mark, the earliest of the four gospels, begins with a prophecy from

Isaiah and then John the Baptizer's appearance, as if from nowhere, in the wilderness and then Jesus' baptism. In Mark the voice from heaven addresses Jesus and tells the reader who he is: "you are my Son, the Beloved." The transcendent perspective given by the heavenly voice in Mark is given to the reader in John through a panoramic view of the whole cosmic picture including God. In this poem the readers are told the story in a condensed, compressed, cryptic form. Readers are transported to the beginning, just as the readers of Genesis 1:1 are taken to the beginning when God began to create.

Ancestors of the Logos—Wisdom

Because the opening poem is set off from the gospel by its poetic structure and its use of the word *Logos*, scholars have asked whether the prologue might have come from another author or literary source before it was adapted for the beginning of the gospel. The prologue that introduces the gospel would be another example, along with the double ending, of a history of composition of the gospel. Where did the Johannine community derive this cosmic perspective and this language of Logos in which to understand Jesus? Many theories have been proposed. Some Stoic philosophers of the time used *Logos* to mean the rational principle holding the universe together, and some scholars have seen philosophy behind the prologue. Others see biblical allusions to the speech of God in the prophets and the law.

One of the closest parallels to the language of *Logos* used in the prologue is the Jewish figure of Wisdom, Sophia, who is described in the Old Testament books of Proverbs, Sirach, and the Wisdom of Solomon. These books now appear in the Apocrypha, and in the first century were well-known Jewish writings in Greek. It is likely that the authors of John understood the story of Jesus in the language and imagery of this female figure of Wisdom whom people are urged to seek and desire and who herself yearns to find a home among mortals. She was present with God at creation, and in some texts is described as a master craftsman. She comes to earth to dwell, finds no home, and returns to heaven. She travels the streets and squares, teaching and inviting passersby to eat the food she has to offer and to drink her wine. She seeks to reconcile humans with God and make them "friends of God." This summary of the qualities, character, and career of Sophia is based on many Jewish texts about Wisdom from the wisdom tradition of Hebrew Scripture. Reflection of Sophia was not done like systematic theology, but more like story telling, poetry, and exhortation.

The best way to get a sense of the figure of wisdom is to read the texts in which she is described. Historical scholars of religion would put the matter this way: early Christians found the Jewish myth of Wisdom as creative force and mediator between God and human to be a compelling way to understand Jesus' ministry, crucifixion, and resurrection. For readers of John today, hearing the allusions of Wisdom in the gospel enriches faithful understanding of this gospel by linking it more closely with Jewish traditions of Torah as the means of knowing God. Hearing them recalls and highlights many traditional ways of imagining the divine as a woman and emphasizes the close kinship between Jesus/Logos/Wisdom and the creation/cosmos/world.

Jewish Texts about Wisdom
- Prov 1:20–33
- Prov 3:13–18
- Prov 4:1–9
- Prov 8:1–36
- Prov 9:1–6
- Wis 7:21–8:1 (Apocrypha)
- Sir 24:1–22 (Apocrypha)

This poetic introduction to the gospel with its long-distance perspective and its ecstatic affirmation—"we have seen his glory"—is in many ways complete in itself. The episodes that follow narrate traditions about Jesus' life and teaching that resemble, more closely than the prologue, the content of the other gospels. The prologue lays out the essential choice for the readers of the gospel: to receive or not receive the *Logos*, to believe or not in his name. The opening prologue matches in tone and theme the first ending of the gospel, "these were written so that you might believe and believing you might have life in his name." The Jesus story will be another way of talking about the entry of the Logos into the cosmos, whose purpose is to lead people to life.

Creation and Wisdom in the Story of the Word

In my comments on the story of the prologue, I will highlight echoes of the story of Wisdom in the story of the Word and in the rest of the gospel. I will also draw attention to themes of creation which run throughout John. The crisis that generates some of the prodigious energy of this gospel is the tragedy expressed in the verse: "He came to what was his own, and his own people did not accept him." This tragic rejection so strains the connection between Jesus and his own, that, in the view of the authors of the gospel, the link between God and the world can be severed. When this bond is cut, the language of dualism between the world and humanity becomes most harsh, as in Jesus' prayer to God about his disciples in John 17:14: "I have given them your word, and the world has hated them because they do not belong to the world, just as I do not belong to the world."

When the rejection is accepted as permanent and irredeemable, it is a short step to identifying those who reject Jesus with enemies of God. The cycle of rejection and exclusion, damnation and violence is played out in John in living color, particularly in its portrait of the unbelieving Jews. An utterly tragic interpretation of the story of Jesus in John leads to an exclusive reading, a temptation to respond to the song of praise and promise in the prologue with rejection of those who do not accept. However, when one takes seriously the gospel's portrayal of the close kinship of creation with Jesus, then it is more difficult to conclude that exclusion is permanent and the solution final.

An utterly tragic interpretation of the story of Jesus in John leads to an exclusive reading, a temptation to respond to the song of praise and promise in the prologue with rejection of those who do not accept.

The creation of all things through the Logos is the key first moment in the plot of the drama synopsized in the prologue. The Logos, called light, and witnessed by John, comes into the cosmos. The beginning, the ground, the origin of the drama of this gospel is the kinship of the Logos with the creation of all things (*ta panta*). The Logos is God's companion and co-worker in creation much as Wisdom is in Proverbs 8:22: "The Lord created me at the beginning of his work, the first of his acts of long ago. Ages ago I was set up, at the first, before the beginning of the earth." Logos, like Wisdom, brings life (Sir 1:4, 4:12) and light. As God first created Light, so light shining in the darkness is the image for creation, for the presence of the Logos. The fact that nothing was made without the Logos prepares readers for the rest of the gospel in which the Creator is in ongoing relationship with creation through wine, water, bread, light, shepherd, and vine.

All of the signs that Jesus provides speak of his engagement with the created world and its goodness. At the wedding Jesus transforms water into wine and provides joy for the feast. He offers never-ending living water to the woman of Samaria. He promises the official that his son will live, restores creation on the Sabbath day for the man at the pool, and feeds bread of life to the people in abundance. He calls himself the light of the world, and like God in the garden makes mud to heal the eyes of the man born blind. He gives life to Lazarus. In all these signs he continues his creative work, not only showing his "power" as creator over the elements, water, earth, food, but providing food, drink, healing, and life to human beings.

> In all these signs he continues his creative work, not only showing his "power" as creator over the elements, water, earth, food, but providing food, drink, healing and life to human beings.

Allusions to both creation stories in Genesis run through John, from the signs to the discourses to the Easter appearances. The resurrection stories affirm creation by alluding to Genesis 1 and 2. The garden in which Jesus is buried and where Mary seeks him when she visits evokes the garden in Genesis 2 as well as the garden in the Song of Songs. When Jesus appears to the disciples in the evening and greets them, he breathes on them, just as Yahweh breathes into the dust creature the breath of life (Gen 2:7). And in the last appearance told by the gospel, Jesus provides a large catch of fish, too many at first to pull in, one hundred and fifty three of them, an evocation of the swarming waters of Genesis 1:21, the plenitude and variety of creatures in the sea. The affirmation that nothing that was made was made without the Logos also means that nothing that was made lacks connection with the divine. If John is a "spiritual" gospel then spiritual must relate the spirit with the created order.

Trouble in the World for the Word

The second movement of the drama of the Logos is the coming of the Word into the world (*kosmos*). In the gospel this coming is imagined as a descent from the Father. Other Christological hymns in the

New Testament describe this descent as an emptying or a renuncia-
tion of status (Phil 2:6–11). In the first verse of the third stanza, the
hymn repeats the close association of the Logos with the kosmos—
the Logos is present in the world and the kosmos came into being
through him and then makes the statement that the kosmos did not
know or recognize him. Why this is so is the unsolved mystery of the
gospel. Verse 11 repeats this strange contrast and unexpected
response in a more personal way: "To his own he came, and his own
people did not accept him."

The figure of Wisdom is likewise described as yearning for
humanity, wanting to be sought and found, and yet not finding a
home on earth. She speaks in the first person in Sirach 24:6–7: "Over
the waves of the sea, over all the earth, and over every people and
nation I have held sway. Among all these I sought a resting place; in
whose territory should I abide?" The most explicit parallel text about
Wisdom's descent and return is in Enoch 42:2: "Wisdom came to
make her dwelling place among the children of men and found no
dwelling place." In contrast, in the story in John the Logos does dwell
with "us." The phrase translated "to his own" (*eis ta idia*) has layers
of meaning. In the mythological story of the Word and Creation, it
means "those created by him." It may refer to those who were human
flesh as the Word became. And in the story of Jesus, the historical
figure, it may mean his own people, his family or the Jewish people.
If the phrase "his own did not accept him" refers to Jesus' crucifixion, it is a very oblique and general way to speak of Jesus' passion.

The overall failure of Jesus' public ministry is narrated in John
1–12, the section called by Raymond Brown "The Book of Signs." Like
Wisdom who cries out in the street to passersby "to eat of my bread,
and drink of the wine I have mixed," Jesus executes a series of public
signs and teaching. Although he has success in Samaria through the
apostolic witness of the Samaritan woman, his signs create opposition and persecution (5:16) after healing the man on the Sabbath,
after the Bread of Life sermon (6:52), at the Festival of Booths, after
the healing of the man born blind, and the raising of Lazarus. The
final words of this section express Jesus' lack of success: "Although
he had performed so many signs in their presence, they did not
believe in him (12:37). In Mark's tale of this public ministry, enor-

mous crowds acclaim Jesus and poor, faithful ones recognize him. In Luke, miracles bring people to faith. Like other gospels, John cites the prophecy from Isaiah 53:1 to explain that it is God's will that they not understand. The use of this prophecy by the gospel writers probably represented later reflection on the lack of acceptance of Jesus as Messiah by the majority of Jews. The readers of the gospel are encouraged to oppose those who do not believe and to identify themselves with those who accept Jesus.

Immediately following the emphatic repeated statements about the failure of the Word to be accepted, which corresponds to the public ministry in John 1–12, comes the focus of attention of the hymn: for those who *do* accept him "he gave power to become children of God." The second part of the gospel, beginning at John 13:1, what Raymond Brown calls the "Book of Glory," begins with the anointing by Mary of Bethany and continues at the foot-washing supper and farewell discourse. This section illustrates the character of the relationship between Jesus and those whom he loves among the friends. Verse 1:12, which English translations begin with contrasting conjunction, "but" is the hinge of the hymn. It is in the emphatic position at the midpoint of the chiastic structure.

The gospel uses different images to describe what we would call "salvation." This one is distinctive because it describes the Logos as giving those who accept him and believe in his name "authority" to become children of God. The word translated, "power," *exousia* describes "empowerment." The phrase "children of God" speaks of new identity and new relationship, a being born in a new way. The new family is another way of speaking about the "friends of God" described by Jesus at the last supper.

Logos Becomes Flesh; Logos Pitches a Tent Among Us

The final stanza is remarkable for the images it uses to describe the Logos' advent to the world: "became flesh (*sarx egeneto*) and "lived among us" (*eskenosen*) and for the surprising shift to the first person plural, "us" and "we." Having narrated the previous stanza in an impersonal, biblical, omniscient tone, at this point the narrator becomes visible and audible, and the reader becomes aware that there is a "we" who is the source for the previous information and a "we" who have become God's children. Although some have proposed that the "we" is Peter, James, and John, the disciples who according to the synoptic gospels were present on the mountain when Jesus was transfigured, and "seeing his glory" refers to that event, it is more consistent with the Fourth Gospel's view of authority and leadership to understand that the "we" is the unnamed ones who are testifying to the truth of the Jesus events in the book. At the same time, the authoritative "we" includes the readers of the book who accept the Logos and have faith in his name. These "we" affirmations are climactic, celebratory, even ecstatic, like a chorus that concludes this hymn to Christ as God.

These "we" affirmations are climactic, celebratory, even ecstatic, like a chorus that concludes this hymn to Christ as God.

With the statement "The Word became flesh and lived among us" the hymn most concretely and specifically speaks of the Jesus of history who will be the protagonist of the gospel. While "he came to what was his own, and his own people did not accept him " is a more distant, mythological way of talking about the Word's coming to the world (kosmos), "the word became flesh" speaks of what we know as the doctrine of the "incarnation," literally the "becoming flesh." "Flesh" (*sarx*) has more graphic and realistic connotations than "he came" and this formulation does not have parallels in the story of Wisdom nor in philosophical speculation. The Johannine community interpreted the story of Jesus as the creator of all things, the Logos, now becoming flesh. This is the second time in the hymn that the noun *logos* is used after its first appearance in the opening lines. The noun connects verse 1 with verse 14 and reminds the reader that it is God who is becoming flesh.

The phrase "and lived among us" completes the assertion that the Word became flesh. The word "eskenosen" translated, "lived" literally means "tented," "camped out," as in "pitched a tent." The word resonates with biblical allusions. Exodus tells that Israel makes a tent for God to dwell with God's people. The prophets imagined that God would make his dwelling among the people. The woman Wisdom makes her tent among humans:

"Then the Creator of all things gave me a command and my Creator chose the place for my tent. He said, 'Make your dwelling in Jacob and in Israel receive your inheritance.' . . . In the holy tent I ministered before him, and so I was established in Zion" (Sir 24:8, 10).[15]

The root of "to tent," *skenao*, is the same root as that of Shekinah, a term used by the rabbis to speak of the presence of God. Here the prologue speaks of Jesus as God's Shekinah.

The author of Revelation is the other New Testament author who uses this verb. In Revelation 7:15 and in 21:3, "He will dwell (tent) with them, and they shall be His People." Pitching a tent makes sense in a context of wandering people who regularly break camp and move to another location. Being able to pitch a tent means being mobile rather than fixed. A tent is at once a potentially temporary dwelling and a dwelling whose location was chosen and not predetermined. Tenting is not a permanent home—it may or may not imply that another permanent home lies elsewhere. The Gospel of John will play with these ideas with the verb *meno*, which means to remain, abide, or dwell. As the gospel unfolds it will be seen how the visit of the Logos has profound implications for where God dwells now. God not only dwelt with "us" in the past, in the history told in the gospel, but dwells, abides with us in the present in the community taught by the Paraclete. This sense of the ongoing present dwelling of God with us hovers over all the stories in John, even the ones which appear to relate the past. A scholarly technical term for this theological perspective is "realized eschatology." Another way to speak of it is that God's gift of life is given in the present in the community, the tent of God in the world.

Eschatology: the branch of theology that concerns itself with the end of time

"We have seen his glory" is a climactic announcement. The Sinai traditions of the Old Testament describe the presence of God as "glory" (*doxa*, *kabod*). The "we" claims to have seen his glory, and this vision is the inspiration for the gospel. His seen glory is not restricted to the glory at the Transfiguration, but the glory of the Word shines out from every page of the gospel, from the wedding at Cana forward. The gospel will convey the texture of that glory through the poeticized and detailed stories of Jesus' ministry. "Come and see" is the invitation of Philip to his companion and the woman of Samaria to her townspeople. The gospel will not only report, but will replicate that experience of seeing. The lavish phrase "grace upon grace" is in the style of doxology and celebration. The final line of the hymn, perhaps an editorial expansion, seems to back off a bit from the confident, "we have seen his glory." It contrasts Moses' not seeing God face to face with the intimate connection of the Son, close to the Father's heart.

Doxology: any of several hymns or praise to God; a) the greater doxology, which begins Gloria in excelsis Deo (glory to God in the highest); b) the lesser doxology, which begins Gloria Patri (glory to the Father); c) a hymn beginning "Praise God from whom all blessings flow"

The prologue sings of God as Logos coming to dwell with his own. It tells of trouble during the sojourn of the Word. The hymn promises power to be children of God for those who receive and believe, and it rejoices in a vision of glory. Woven into the hymn are explanatory comments dealing with the status of John, witness to the Light, and Moses, giver of the Law. The kinship of the creation with the Logos is emphasized by the allusions to the biblical story of creation in the prologue and in the gospel as a whole.

Continuing the Conversation . . .

The literature on the prologue is vast. For a detailed treatment see the volumes cited above, esp. Raymond Brown, *The Gospel According to John*, Anchor *Bible Commentary* (New York: Doubleday, 1966–1970).

For discussion of the prologue and the gospel as a whole, see L. William Countryman, *The Mystical Way in the Fourth Gospel: Crossing Over in God* (Valley Forge, Pa.: Trinity Press, 1994).

On themes of Wisdom in the prologue and throughout the gospel, see Sharon Ringe, *Wisdom's Friends: Community and Christology in the Fourth Gospel* (Louisville: Westminster John Knox Press, 1999).

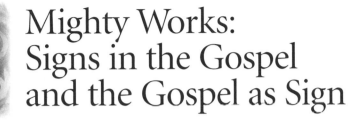

CHAPTER THREE

Mighty Works:
Signs in the Gospel
and the Gospel as Sign

*Your mighty works reveal your wisdom
and love.*

BCP 373

All the gospels are persuasive religious literature that
seeks to communicate the character and import of Jesus,
the gospel's subject and hero. The Gospel of John highlights this communicative function by calling Jesus' mighty
deeds "signs." Jesus himself speaks of them as his "works,"
a term which links his deeds with the "works" of God in
creation as in God's wondrous works praised in Psalm 107.
The word "sign" (from the Greek *semeion*) indicates that
its purpose is to *show*, to be a sign of or toward something
beyond itself. Any commentary will tell you that the signs
that Jesus does primarily communicate his "identity." The
word "identity" is abstract, and many answers to the question of identity can be answered with another word, "Messiah," "Son of God," "Rabbi," "Lamb of God." But the signs
communicate more than simply rational information as
in an answer to a question. The signs speak of why Jesus is
significant and why his identity matters to human beings.

Not only are signs the important way that the Fourth
Gospel communicates, but the gospel itself can be understood to be a sign of Jesus. Its purpose is to evoke a
response of faith in its readers. These signs are written

"that you may believe." In the church we understand that the sacraments, Holy Eucharist and baptism, are outward and visible "signs" of an inward and spiritual grace. But in John, "signs" are not identical to the sacraments. The connotations of signs in John are far-ranging and rich and can help us to appreciate neglected dimensions of the sacrament of the Eucharist. John helps us to imagine a Christian community whose central images were wilderness feeding and farewell foot-washing. In the signs Jesus reveals his glory in concrete and material ways.

Are the Signs "Miracles"?

The signs of Jesus in John may be compared with the stories of Jesus' healing and feeding told in Matthew, Mark, and Luke that are commonly called "miracles." A number of the sequence of signs in John 2–12 appear to be versions of the stories of power in the other gospels. Some scholars have proposed that one of the sources for the gospel might be a document consisting of a series of signs, much like the "miracle collection," which the writers of the synoptic gospels adapted in their gospels.[16] The signs in John's story of Jesus' public ministry are:

1. Jesus changes water into wine at Cana.
2. Jesus cures the royal official's son at Cana.
3. Jesus cures a paralyzed person at the pool at Bethsaida.
4. Jesus feeds the five thousand from five loaves and two fishes.
5. Jesus walks on the sea to the disciples and announces "I am."
6. Jesus gives sight to a man born blind.
7. Jesus raises Lazarus from the dead.

Sometimes what Jesus does provokes controversy when the crowds react, and in some cases Jesus argues with, corrects, and teaches those gathered who see the sign. The content of these signs is the same as in Mark, Matthew, and Luke where Jesus heals the sick, raises Jairus' daughter, and makes the blind see. But the way they are told is more elaborate. As they have been retold and interpreted by the Johannine community, these stories have picked up details, turns of phrase, dialogue, and teaching that have made them much more complex than factual accounts of an amazing deed of Jesus. These stories have been transformed into multilayered sermons or vividly painted icons that *reveal* or communicate the divine in a way that the discursive simply cannot.

When we call these events "miracles" and emphasize that they are deeds which defy the laws of nature, we actually miss the point of the event as the evangelists understand it. The synoptic gospels do not use the term "miracles" either, but "deeds of power." People who see the deeds do not exclaim, "He violated the laws of nature!" but ask:

- "Does this power come from God or Satan?"
- "What is the power being used for?"
- "What does power in this man mean that God is doing?"

In the Gospel of Mark, for example, Jesus' exorcising demons from people shows that in Jesus God is battling Satan, and Satan is being overthrown. In Mark's language, the kingdom of God is coming near. By the time the Gospel of John is composed, these stories have developed additional layers of significance which reflect the theological perspective of this community. John does not use "kingdom of God" terminology, because John understands that in Jesus, the Word has come and revealed the Father to the world. Thus, the signs are not communicating something exciting about the near future, but something real and true about the present. In John's language, the signs communicate Jesus' "glory."

One can think of the miracle stories in the gospel as stories with a long history of being told and retold, performed and celebrated. The growing faith of those who told them has shaped the stories. The followers of Jesus understood more and more the impact of Jesus' resurrection in their communal life. Their relationship with their neighbors changed as the wars with Rome and the wrecking of the Temple threw trusted ways of worshipping into chaos. Gentiles came into the fold of believers. All these experiences added layers of meaning to these stories.

The history of the stories begins with Jesus in his lifetime healing the sick and exorcising demons. He demonstrated power through these deeds, power which made his teaching more convincing. When followers of other religious teachers and philosophers taught about them, they too told stories of power. As the stories were repeated they became more resonant and took on symbolic coloring that reflected the changes in the community. The process begins in the synoptic gospels, for example, when Mark's stilling of the storm becomes in Matthew a picture of the boat of the church struggling under adversity (Mark 4:35–41; Matt 8:3–27). In John this process has accelerated, been refined, and become more self-conscious, so that the author can speak of these deeds, in explicitly symbolic terms, as "signs."

The Enigma of Signs

As a symbolic or indirect means of communication, Jesus' signs have irony built into them. While you would think that a sign might be a big, convincing, unmistakable message that anyone could understand, it is clear in the story of John that Jesus' signs cannot be read by everyone. For some people the signs conceal instead of reveal. Some understand them only in part and for some they appear dangerous or even diabolical. This enigmatic quality of signs—that they prove to be divisive—lends to the suspense and drama of the plot of the first half of the gospel. Characters respond to signs in positive, negative, and ambivalent ways. This dynamic underscores the tragedy alluded to in the prologue—"He came to what was his own, and his own people did not accept him." The responses of the various characters to signs speak to the issue of how this community relates to its neighbors. The challenge that signs pose speaks to a reality about spiritual truths. Truths about God are not straightforwardly accessible, but must be communicated by indirect means, a medium that can be misunderstood as easily as comprehended.

How are Signs Spiritual?

Before attending in detail to two signs in John, I want to stress two points about signs in John's gospel in response to misunderstandings I often encounter. The first point is that the gospel is overwhelmingly positive about signs as a means of or as a way to faith. Although there are moments when Jesus appears to criticize "signs faith," such as John 2:23–24—"Many believed in his name because they saw the signs he was doing, but Jesus . . . would not commit himself to them . . ." —the gospel overall relies on signs to show Jesus' glory and wants signs to be effective for those who see them. The first ending says that "these signs were written so that you may believe." In John there is relatively little polemic against signs faith. It may be that modern people have heard a lot of preaching against "faith dependent on miracles" and are less familiar with (or cannot see) John's enthusiastic association of signs with faith. Most important to John is *what* the signs communicate about Jesus, *what* the one who sees understands, and *how* they respond. In the second half of the gospel (John 13–21) after the Book of Signs, Jesus addresses at length and in different figures of speech and action those who respond with faith to the signs. He teaches and illustrates what that response of faith looks like in the community.

The second common misunderstanding about Jesus' signs is that they are symbolic and not literal, or symbolic and not material. The opposite is true; they are symbolic *and* literal, symbolic *and* material. This point flows from the idea stressed in chapter 2 that the Logos is the one "through whom all things were made." The glory of God is revealed through concrete stuff of the material world— water, bread, mud, saliva, sickness, death—and not despite it. The guests really did keep drinking good wine, the official's son really did recover, and Lazarus really did live to have dinner the next day. Sometimes it is difficult to appreciate the concrete aspect of the signs, both because of their clearly symbolic quality and because they are narrated in a rather cold or impersonal manner, as appropriate to their symbolic, iconic nature. Jesus displays little emotion— "he was born blind so that God's works might be revealed in him" (9:3)—so there is little detail to sentimentalize. But the signs work through creation, not in spite of it. To hold the symbolic and literal together, the spiritual and corporeal in tandem, is the key to doing justice to the expansive foundation of this gospel.

Wine and Bread from Nowhere out of Almost Nothing

In two signs in John, Jesus provides for his people. One, the wedding at Cana, is found in no other gospel, and the other, the feeding of the multitude and the walking on water, is found in Luke and in two versions in Matthew and Mark. We will look in detail at these stories to see how they work as signs, what they show of Jesus and right response to him, and how they hold together the spiritual and physical. Both the story of Cana, with the central motif of wine, and the story of the wilderness feeding, with the central image of bread, have been read as reference to the sacrament of the Eucharist. Rather than reduce these signs to ciphers for the Eucharist, I will show how the wedding feast and the picnic in the wilderness include a eucharistic dimension but encompass a richer and wider range of meaning.

GOOD WINE AT THE WEDDING—THE FIRST OF JESUS' SIGNS

Manifest at Jordan's stream, Prophet, Priest, and King supreme;
and at Cana, wedding guest, in thy Godhead manifest;
manifest in power divine, changing water into wine;
anthems be to thee addressed, God in man made manifest.

CHRISTOPHER WORDSWORTH (1807–1885) HYMNAL 1982, 135

The words that conclude the story of an unusual wedding show that it is not just a story but a revelation. Worshippers in the East commemorated this episode at the feast of the Epiphany, and it makes good sense that this story inaugurates a season of showing: "Jesus did this, the first of his signs, at Cana in Galilee, and revealed his glory; and his disciples believed in him" (2:11). Whatever happened at Cana takes prominence as the first of Jesus' signs, and it is said to reveal his glory, glory that has been spoken of in the prologue, "and we have seen his glory." In the statement that precedes this sign, Jesus speaks of a vision of passage between heaven and earth, "you will see heaven opened and the angels of God ascending and descending upon the Son of Man" (1:51). The event is revelatory; it evokes belief among the disciples assembled in Galilee and present at the wedding.

This first sign of Jesus' glory is a highly developed symbolic story whose details and odd sequence communicate less realistically and more symbolically. It is hard to answer questions about the text that assume that the story works rationally, questions such as:

n Who is getting married?
n Why were the disciples and Jesus' mother invited?

- Why did the wine run out?
- Why is Jesus impolite to his mother?
- Why were there huge stone jars at a wedding reception?

To understand what and how the sign reveals it is more promising to ask:

- What is the significance of a wedding for revealing Jesus' glory?
- How do you decipher the meaning of "My hour is not yet come"?
- What exactly is the "miracle" in the story and who sees it?

The preamble to the marriage service in the Book of Common Prayer rehearses the traditional teaching, "our Lord Jesus Christ adorned this manner of life by his presence and first miracle at a wedding in Cana of Galilee" (BCP 423). Within the story itself, as it stands in John, there is no implication that Jesus blessed marriage by being at this wedding; he and his family and friends were simply there. The importance of the wedding setting is that a wedding banquet was a prophetic image of the time of fulfillment, a messianic time: "On this mountain the LORD of hosts will make for all peoples a feast of rich food, a feast of well-aged wines, of rich food filled with marrow, of well-aged wines strained clear" (Isa 25:6).

A marriage feast is a time of consummation and joy. A thread of nuptial imagery runs through John, a filament that is often hidden in popular interpretation. It is the imagery of wooing, seeking, and finding common to the Song of Songs and to language about the human and divine relationship. John the Baptist compares himself to the friend of the bridegroom, the supporting role at a wedding. The woman of Samaria and Jesus converse at a well, a place of engagements, and Mary seeks the crucified Jesus in a garden. To open the public ministry of Jesus with a wedding feast is to show that the action of the gospel will take place within this wider symbolic system of weddings, attendants, guests, hosts, servants, food, and drink in which a marriage is a symbol for consummation, *and* that Jesus and his friends participate fully in the social fabric and network of the village of Cana.

At public celebrations, wine is a necessary ingredient, expressing joy and fellowship. To lack wine, to run out of it at a feast, is a serious problem, as serious for a feast like this as being hungry or thirsty in the desert is for wanderers or being tossed in a small boat in a storm at sea is for sailors. The mother of Jesus informs him of the emergency. She appears twice in this gospel, once here at the opening of his ministry and at the cross where Jesus commits her into the keeping of the beloved disciple and him to her: "When Jesus saw his mother and the disciple whom he loved standing beside her, he said to his mother, 'Woman, here is your son.' Then he said to the disciple, 'Here is your mother.' And from that hour the disciple took her into his own home" (John 19:26–27).

These two moments take on an extraordinary significance, because in each the mother of Jesus has a symbolic or representative role. In the first she participates in the event that reveals Jesus' glory, and in the second Jesus creates between his mother and the disciple whom he loves the family which will abide after his death. In light of that scene, here at the wedding, Jesus' strange remark to her may be better understood: "Woman, what concern is that to you and to me? My hour has not yet come" (2:4). The "hour" becomes a quasi-technical term referring to the hour of his death when he will be lifted up to the Father and draw all people to himself. It appears that Jesus is initially resisting her implied request with a reference to his ultimate sign of glory. But somehow between her transmission of information, his rebuff, and her instructions to the servants, it is decided that a need will be met and glory will be revealed now and not delayed. To push this gap in the text too far and insist on asking, "Why did Jesus change his mind?" or "What was her exact role in this decision?" is to try to answer a question that the text leaves opaque.

To lack wine, to run out of it at a feast, is a serious problem, as serious for a feast like this as being hungry or thirsty in the desert is for wanderers or being tossed in a small boat in a storm at sea is for sailors.

At the instruction of the mother, the servants comply with Jesus, who asks them to fill the stone jars with water to the brim, take some out, and take it to the steward. The narrator's explanation that the stone jars are used for Jewish rites of purification both draws attention to their original use, which will be implicitly contrasted with the use Jesus' sign makes of them, and expresses distance between this community to whom the narrator is speaking and the Jewish rites explained in the description.

In miracle stories there is often an acclamation where the witnesses affirm the event with words like, "we have never seen anything like this! (Mark 2:12) or "a great prophet has arisen among us!" (Luke 7:16). The only acclamation here is given by the steward. We don't know what the guests said, or Jesus' mother, or the disciples. The acclamation is given in the form of a proverb, and what he says is very interesting. He doesn't say, "Wow, this wine used to be water!" as

For the servants the "miracle" is the transformation of water to wine; for the steward the miracle is in the timing of the provision of excellent wine.

we might expect the servants to say or the thirsty guests, but says something that only someone who had actually tasted the wine and who remembered the flavor of the wine that was gone: "Everyone serves the good wine first, and then the inferior wine after the guests have become drunk. But you have kept the good wine until now!" (2:10) For the servants the "miracle" is the transformation of water to wine; for the steward the miracle is in the timing of the provision of excellent wine. In one way this reaction shows lack of understanding on his part, and on another level accurate knowledge that the best is now last, an unexpected and utterly impractical strategy for a host.

The disciples who have presumably seen this event and the readers understand that Jesus has here revealed his glory—that the messianic time of fulfillment has indeed arrived, that the best wine has been saved until now, and that Jewish rites of purification have become obsolete in this new age of banqueting. All these realizations and meanings are hidden within the story and cannot simply be discursively announced as information. All these theological or spiritual dimensions are part of what Jesus' glory means, but Jesus' glory also means something very concrete. Jesus' glory means that Jesus provides wine when it is needed. Jesus gives an abundance of wine, one hundred and twenty gallons, even if the guests are already inebriated, and Jesus gives an abundance of excellent wine, *kalon oinon.* Wine is wine. At the same time, wine is a symbol of Jesus' gifts to human beings of joy and life, grace upon grace.

The first sign confirms that Jesus is the Logos made flesh who provides from creation and engenders life and joy. The confirmation does not come in the language of myth and poetry as in the prologue, but in the story of friends in a village. Like Wisdom, Jesus offers wine and food as a gracious host who invites people to feast:

> "Come, eat of my bread and drink of the wine I have mixed. Lay aside immaturity and live, and walk in the way of insight." (Prov 9:5–6)

> "Come to me all you who desire me, and eat the fill of my fruits. For the memory of me is sweeter than honey, and the possession of me sweeter than the honeycomb. Those who eat of me will hunger for more, and those who drink of me will thirst for more." (Sir 24:19–21)

This first sign *is* a sign of Jesus' identity, but this identity is rooted in the stuff of creation, the water, the wine, and the marriage among friends. The sign of the provision of excellent wine late in the party illustrates, fills out, and gives texture to the concrete glory of Jesus.

CAN GOD SPREAD A TABLE IN THE WILDERNESS? (PSALM 78:19)

Gracious Father, whose blessed Son Jesus Christ came down from heaven to be the true bread which giveth life to the world: Evermore give us this bread, that he may live in us, and we in him; who liveth and reigneth with thee and the Holy Spirit, one God, now and for ever. Amen.

COLLECT FOR THE FOURTH SUNDAY IN LENT, BCP 167

The two signs of feeding and walking on the sea with their accompanying dialogue and discourse are fine examples of the process of elaboration from deed of power to Johannine sign. The story of a generous wilderness feeding from very little is important to Mark, Matthew, and Luke, and there the story incorporates the liturgical rhythm of the practice of the Eucharist—blessed, broke, gave—which is part of the community's worship. John tells the story of feeding with specific details from his tradition, like the barley loaves and the young boy, and like the other evangelists tells it back to back with a storm story. In John, however, after the sea-sign Jesus argues with the quizzical crowd, and then delivers a multi-part sermon about the bread of life. One element of the feeding story—the bread—becomes the subject of a detailed homily with its own distinctive movement. The sermon does not develop other elements of the feeding story, such as the fish or the storm, but focuses in on bread from a variety of angles. The movement of the passage progresses from broadest to most narrow:

1. Jesus gives bread.
2. I am bread.
3. Eat my flesh.

Jesus' giving of bread in the opening scene is well-received by the crowd but, as the sermon progresses, those around have more and more difficulty accepting it. The crowd's ambivalence matches the progression from a well-known tradition of Jesus to more and more radically particular teaching of Jesus about himself. It is as though the teaching in the discourse becomes more and more esoteric and therefore more divisive. Notice how the sermon that follows the sign is more combative than the sign itself, and that Jesus is very critical of the response of the crowd to the sign. This movement may realistically portray increasing opposition to Jesus as beliefs "about" him become more and more particularly defined. Of all the meals in John: the wedding, the meal in the desert, dinner at Mary and Martha's house, the supper when Jesus washes the feet of his friends, and the breakfast on the beach, this one is the only one that is so hostile and disagreeable. It is the only one that is open to the public and to which the public responds ambivalently at best. Jesus demands more and more specific beliefs and practices, and appears to lose people in the process. Hearing this story would be reassuring to those who already understand and accept the specific beliefs and practices and would vividly illustrate their rejection by others.

PROPHET FEEDS THE HUNGRY IN THE DESERT

All the stories of the feeding of the multitude in the gospels have been shaped by the church's eucharistic practice, but in John the parallels with the Eucharist are looser than in the other gospels. Jesus does not break the loaves and he does not give the food to the disciples to distribute. Important details in John's version of the story associate the feeding with the Passover (6:4) and link Jesus' role here more closely with Moses, the leader of the people who fed them with manna in the wilderness and to whom they dangerously grumbled. The high cost of buying food is contrasted with the meager lunch of the small boy. Like the Cana story where the guests have more than ample wine, in this sign the people eat "as much as they wanted" and later are said to have "eaten their fill." Twelve baskets of left-over fragments are gathered up. Both stories convey divine plenty and generosity.

The wilderness feeding story in John is the closest this author comes to narrating the institution of the Eucharist, and even so the echoes are gentle rather than explicit. In the Fourth Gospel, during the last meal that Jesus spends with his disciples before his death, he does not command his friends to eat the bread and drink the cup "in remembrance of me" but to wash each other's feet, "For I have set you an example, that you also should do as I have done to you" (13:15). So, in John the "Eucharist" happens in the wilderness near the beginning with a crowd rather than at the supper at the end among disciples.

Some scholars of this gospel have seen this important divergence from the synoptic tradition as an indication that the Johannine community was somehow critical of the sacrament of the Eucharist as the church had begun to perform it. However, to my mind this Johannine "wrinkle" in what we now know had become "tradition" is suggestive. The meanings hovering around this meal are those of manna provided by God in the wilderness wanderings of the people of Israel. Jesus resembles the prophet Moses who struggles to lead the people, who are subject to serious mood swings, safely to the promised land. In this story bread is a sustaining food in a way that it is not in the institution narrative: "this is my body." In 1 Corinthians 10:1–5 Paul refers to the wilderness traditions and the Eucharist when he says that our ancestors "all ate the same spiritual food and all drank the same spiritual drink." This text is evidence that early traditions connected the Jesus community with the wilderness generation. The author elaborates upon the elements of Moses and manna later in the sermon (6:25–34). It may be that the community of John's gospel reflected on the suppers of Jesus in light of a different assembly of Scriptures than the communities of Mark, Matthew, and Luke. Or it may be that its meal practice developed a bit differently. This Johannine variation in the placement of the Eucharist traditions and on the symbolic act of the final supper is another way that the Fourth Gospel holds the canon open. Its non-conformity is initially disorienting, but ultimately enriching.

"I AM LORD OF SEA AND LAND"—SELF-REVELATION ON THE SEA

After the feeding story and before the sermon, the gospel narrates the story of Jesus walking on the sea during a storm. Because a sea-walking story follows the feeding stories in Mark, scholars surmise that these two deeds of power were paired with one another in the tradition that lies behind both Mark and John. The ideas of God's power over the water and God's pro- **Midrash:** an early Jewish vision of the food in the wilderness mediated interpretation of or com- through Moses link the two stories. Here in John mentary on a biblical text the most important line is Jesus' identification of himself. On one level, his statement is simply a reassuring answer to the disciples' terror. On another level it is the first of the great "I am" statements in the gospel, this time without any predicate, as it is in the revelation of God to Moses in the burning bush (Exod 3:14): "I am who I am." This awesome theophany provokes an odd reaction—the disciples wish to take him into the boat with them and an inconclusive and mysterious ending—the boat reaches the land. The sermon that follows does not develop this sign, but rather focuses on bread. It's fun to imagine what an alternative midrash on the sea-walking might be: "I am the sea;" "I am the good sailor;" "I am the one who fishes."

From Sign to Sermon

In the opening remarks in this chapter, I stressed how the sign in John holds together the physical and the spiritual. In the discourse which follows the story of the feeding of the multitude, Jesus' teaching appears to push in a more "spiritual" and less "material" direction as Jesus criticizes the motivation of the crowd's search for Jesus not for seeing signs, but "because you ate your fill of the loaves" (6:26). He contrasts the bread which perishes with the bread that endures for eternal life, as if to push them to a more advanced understanding of bread. As the teaching becomes more specific, it provokes more and more misunderstanding and greater and greater objection. Jesus corrects the idea that Moses gave bread by asserting that "my Father" gave you the bread from heaven. Then to the people's request to give them the bread of God always, Jesus uses the "I am" formula and identifies himself as the bread of life: "I am the bread of life. Whoever comes to me will never be hungry, and whoever believes in me will never be thirsty" (John 6:35).

By speaking in the first person and using the "I am" formulation, Jesus in John echoes the language used in Jewish literature to speak about Wisdom and in the songs of praise which celebrate the Egyptian goddess Isis. Wisdom too promises that her bread and wine fully satisfy. The prophet Isaiah speaks of the Word of God as bread which is effective and life-giving.

> For as the rain and the snow come down from heaven, and do not return there until they have watered the earth, making it bring forth and sprout, giving seed to the sower and bread to the eater, so shall my word be that goes out from my mouth; it shall not return to me empty, but it shall accomplish that which I purpose, and succeed in the thing for which I sent it. (Isa 55:10–11)

All these religious and spiritual streams converge in Jesus' words "I am the bread of life." The parables in the synoptic gospels use the images of bread, yeast, vineyard, and light to convey qualities of the kingdom of God which is dawning. In the "I am" speeches in John, Jesus equates himself with bread, light, and vine. In John the presence and reality of Jesus is important rather than language about the kingdom of God. Rather than the narrator of the gospel telling that Jesus is a descendent of David or behaves like Elijah, Jesus speaks directly of himself. Jesus' style of speaking here may come from the activity of the community prophesying under the influence of the Paraclete or Spirit. They hear the voice of Jesus speaking these words. In reading the "I am" speeches in John, it is fruitful to emphasize both the subject, Jesus, and the predicate, bread, light, vine. For not only do the statements emphasize that Jesus is all these elements, but these elements, the nourishment of bread, the illumination of light, and the fruitfulness of the vine reflect qualities of Jesus.

From Bread to Flesh

The sermon shifts from the language of bread to the language of flesh. The mention of eating and drinking ties this part of the sermon more directly to the sacrament of the Eucharist and appears to provoke and offend even the disciples. Having opened with the broadest understanding of bread as food in the wilderness, the sermon concludes with the narrowest reading of bread, to bread as Jesus' flesh. Jesus even states the situation most negatively: "Very truly, I tell you, unless you eat the flesh of the Son of Man and drink his blood, you have no life in you" (6:53).

Signs in the Gospel and Gospel as Sign

For Anglicans, appreciation of the sacraments comes naturally, since the celebration of the Eucharist is foundational to our spirituality. The role of signs in the Gospel of John can expand our appreciation of the breadth of symbolic and narrative associations of the Eucharist. Not only is it a farewell meal as it is in the synoptics and in Paul, but it is a massive picnic in the wilderness. Not only is the bread Jesus' body, but it is manna from heaven, the bread of angels. Bread is teaching and Torah and Wisdom. The wine is not just Jesus' blood, but the free-flowing drink at the messianic feast, the substance of joy. Word and table are brought together by the image of word as bread.

> *Not only is the bread Jesus' body, but it is manna from heaven, the bread of angels. Bread is teaching and Torah and Wisdom.*

> Shepherd of souls, refresh and bless thy chosen pilgrim flock
> With manna from the wilderness, and water from the rock.
>
> JAMES MONTGOMERY (1771–1854) HYMNAL 1982, 343

Continuing the Conversation . . .

See Robert T. Fortna, *The Fourth Gospel and its Predecessor: From Narrative Source to Present Gospel* (Philadelphia: Fortress, 1998); Craig Koester, *Symbolism in the Fourth Gospel: Meaning, Mystery, Community* (Minneapolis: Fortress, 1995).

Your Father the Devil: Jews and Jewish Tradition in John

The portrayal of the Jews in John as the representatives of human unbelief is one of the most difficult dimensions of the Fourth Gospel. A few years ago during an introductory class on the Gospel of John, to begin to discuss the topic of John's harsh rhetoric, I quoted the author of one of our readings who said something like, "while for some people the Gospel of John is the gospel of love, for some readers, it might be called the gospel of hate." I realized only after the class how upset some of the students in the class were by that remark. They had heard me say that the Gospel of John *is* the gospel of hate and is not the gospel of love. The linking of "hate" with the beloved gospel of the Christian tradition was shocking and deeply troubling to them.

I know now how emotionally difficult it can be to explore the dynamics of hate and love in the Fourth Gospel. First, I will highlight how the gospel portrays the opposition between light and dark, inside and outside, children of light and children of darkness in the movement of the story. While readers familiar with the gospel hear that language as positive and reassuring, it is important to imagine hearing the text as others do, with the ears of Jewish readers or those outside the circle of belief. When we do this, we hear exclusionary rhetoric which has been and continues to be deeply hurtful to our sisters and brothers whom God has made. Furthermore, the same language does something harmful to us, if we use it without care and critical reflection. To respond to the challenge of the prominence of harsh and violent words in sacred Scripture, I will offer some historical information to account for the anti-Jewish polemics. In the final part I will draw attention to stories in the gospel that call into question the unremittingly negative portrait of the Jews, especially the story of the family of Mary, Martha, and Lazarus. I will explore the story of the conversation between the woman of Samaria and Jesus at the well as a vision of mission and reconciliation. I will offer ways to put the language of hate into conversation with the expansive arc of this gospel.

In chapters 7 and 8 of John you see a steadily escalating argument between Jesus and the crowds and with those Jews who had believed in him. It is as though the wrangling that concluded the feeding of the multitude in chapter 6 takes on new intensity. The argument culminates in an exchange between Jesus and the Jews which is infamous for its hostility. At stake is the relationship of Jews to God their father. To their claim, "We are not illegitimate children; we have one father, God himself," Jesus answers:

> "If God were your Father, you would love me, for I came from God and now I am here. I did not come on my own, but he sent me. Why do you not understand what I say? It is because you cannot accept my word. You are from your father the devil, and you choose to do your father's desires. He was a murderer from the beginning and does not stand in the truth, because there is no truth in him. When he lies, he speaks according to his own nature, for he is a liar and the father of lies. But because I tell the truth, you do not believe me. Which of you convicts me of sin? If I tell the truth, why do you not believe me? Whoever is from God hears the words of God. The reason you do not hear them is that you are not from God." (John 8:42–47)

The claim that the father of the Jews is the devil, a murderer and liar, is an extreme denial of their claim to have God as their Father. The logic of this argumentative passage is the same as the logic of the gospel. If you believe in Jesus, you are of the light and if you do not you are of the darkness. As the Jews oppose Jesus in the story, so does the world, or kosmos, who is said to hate Jesus. "The world cannot hate you, but it hates me because I testify against it that its works are evil" (John 7:7). The dualism, the stark contrast between opposites, is expressed in spatial terms: "You are from below, I am from above; you are of this world, I am not of this world" (John 8:23). The reversals of darkness and light, blindness and sight, are summarized in the words that conclude chapter 9, the story of the man born blind: "I came into this world for judgment so that those who do not see may see, and those who do see may become blind" (John 9:39). In passages such as these, the gospel portrays a sharp and irreconcilable opposition between those who believe and those who do not, between Jesus and "the world." Posing such a stringent opposition threatens to contradict the argument I offered in the previous chapters that creation is affirmed by Christ's involvement with the making of "all things." Those who argue that the purpose of John is to draw sharp lines between believers and unbelievers, the saved and the damned, find support in the gospel's dualistic outlook.

A powerful story or rhetorical text causes readers to align themselves with the perspective of the narrator and the heroic characters in the story. A religious text often contains an implied instruction or decision the readers must make on its basis. "Insiders" who read John and who believe in Jesus identify with the positive characters in the drama and identify those who oppose Jesus with their own enemies. To Anglicans or other Christians who read this gospel, hearing such language of enmity might not sound so alarming if you by definition are lining up on the side of light and sight. However, if one imagines hearing this text as one whose religious heritage causes you to identify with the Jews in the text, it sounds very different. It sounds like your God and Father is being defamed. You are being literally "de-legitimized." Adele Reinhartz, a Jewish scholar of John, has described this experience of reading very vividly:

> Thus the Beloved Disciple judges me as "evil" if I reject his gift, that is, if I refuse to believe in Jesus Christ as the Son of God. Conversely, he judges me as "good" if I accept his gift through faith in Jesus as savior. The universalizing language . . . stresses that the gift is offered to me

and to all readers who have ever lived or who will ever live. At the same time, I, and all other readers are to be judged according to response to the gift, and are subject to the consequences of our choice."[17]

Throughout history, the gospel's damning language about the character of "the Jews" has incited and been used to justify violence and discrimination against Jews. When the passion was read on Good Friday in churches in Europe, the violence of the pogroms against Jews intensified.[18] The sins committed in the name of these texts by our Christian ancestors make it necessary for us to struggle with the ethical problems posed by such harsh and uncompromising language.

Pogrom: an organized, often officially encouraged massacre or persecution of a minority group, especially one conducted against Jews

It is not only past crimes against others that makes it necessary to face the language of hate in John's gospel, but what the language of hate does to us. The black and white logic of the gospel is powerfully attractive and motivates people to conversion. But it makes it very easy to consign whole religions or races or political positions to the dark side and put them out of reach of God's grace and truth. Dualism tempts us to project onto the enemy all the sin and weakness that beset us and infect our communities. It can turn us away from repentance and toward vengeance. All these temptations make it urgent to try to understand the language of hate and to be in active and vigorous conversation with it.

Understanding the historical situation of the Johannine community in relationship with its Jewish neighbors at the time of the writing of the gospel can help today's reader appreciate the reasons for the sharp divisions portrayed by the gospel. On one level the Gospel of John tells the story of its own community. Clues in the text have led scholars to postulate that at one time the community experienced a severe break with the larger Jewish society. The narrator explains that the parents of the man born blind evaded Jesus' question about how their son received his sight "because they were afraid of the Jews; for the Jews had already agreed that anyone who confessed Jesus to be the Messiah would be put out of the synagogue" (John 9:22). Authorities did not confess belief "for fear that they

It is not only past crimes against others that makes it necessary to face the language of hate in John's gospel, but what the language of hate does to us.

would be put out of the synagogue (12:42)." Jesus warns "they will put you out of the synagogues (16:2)."

Building upon these references, scholars have theorized that at some point in its history the Johannine community's belief in Jesus as Messiah caused it to be separated from the synagogue, the place where Jews met and read Scripture and prayed together. This traumatic rift, this break in social relations, contributed to the development of a perspective of a sharp division between Jesus and the world, and between the community and "the Jews" which we see played out in the text. The language of enmity against "the Jews" in the gospel reflects the intense feelings of loss and hurt of those who had become socially separated from their kinspeople.

The separation of the Johannine community from its local synagogue was part of the larger development, taking place at the end of the first century and continuing over the next, in which Jesus-believing Jews came to see their movement as one distinct from Jewish identity and not part of it. In this dividing of the ways the Jewish sectarian group gradually became a separate system of belief, Christianity.[19] An older and overly simplistic view of this separation theorized one single moment when all Jesus believers were "expelled" from all synagogues, and saw this moment reflected in the phrases in John which refer to being put out of the synagogue. The process by which rabbinic Judaism and Christian orthodoxy came to define themselves in tension with one another is a complex one. Christian readers should be cautious about using the synagogue expulsion theory to justify the language of enmity as a response to Jewish mistreatment of the community.[20]

Whether or not there was a specific incident in the life of the community that constituted a break with Jewish practice, the severe dualism seems to arise out of some kind of crisis, theological or existential. The black and white, outsider and insider, devil and God perspective of John originates in the unexplained tragedy described in the gospel prologue: "He came to what was his own, and his own people did not accept him."

The rejection of Jesus by humanity or by his Jewish colleagues and the subsequent experience of rejection of the Johannine community begin the cycle of reflection that leads to a dualistic solution.

Wayne Meeks explains this dynamic in his influential essay, "The Man from Heaven in Johannine Sectarianism."[21] The idea that a sect is a select predestined few comes across in some parts of Jesus' prayer at the farewell supper: "I have made your name known to those whom you gave me from the world. They were yours, and you gave them to me, and they have kept your word" (John 17:6). The frustration of an unexplained tragedy can be eased and satisfied by an explanation that some were fated to believe and others were not. Taken to its logical conclusion, such a viewpoint can develop into a radically dualistic perspective in which God, too, is understood to be divided. Some Christian thinkers, among those who have been called "Gnostics," argued in this direction and posited an evil God responsible for creation and a good God revealed in Jesus.

The dialogue between Jesus and the Jews in chapter 8 illustrates the cycle of name calling, blame, and vilification among those who were once close. It is unlikely that this was the typical style of argument for Jesus among his fellow Jews in his lifetime, but the polemics here may reflect charges and countercharges exchanged between Jesus communities and other Jewish groups during the protracted "parting of the ways." One way to read this difficult passage in the gospel is to see it as a horrifying example of failed inclusion or dialogue gone wrong, failed negotiation—not a positive example to be imitated but a cautionary example of failure.

The Gospel of John's anti-Judaism is the most disruptive element to an expansive reading. Conversation with Scripture becomes strained, fervent, even critical. Appreciation of the historical situation helps us to understand the presence and intensity of the polemics, but understanding does not change or excuse them. To change them requires reading differently, seeking different choices than the text itself provides, to help us find respectful ways to be in dialogue with faithful Jews.

One step toward reading differently is to take seriously the strong affirmation at the opening of the gospel of the indissoluble link between Christ and "all things." Without the Logos, nothing was made that was made. Such a claim will not allow denial of the world or its consignment to a realm outside of God. Although in the symbol system of John, Jews are enemies of Jesus, God's commitment to all God has made would not leave them permanently outside. Such a perspective would reflect on the tragedy of non-reception without finding a fatalistic explanation for it: "It had to be that way."

Jewish Family and Neighbors Grieve at Bethany (John 11:1–44)

Another way to read differently is to notice aspects of the text that are exceptions to commonly held truisms about the gospel. The Jewish New Testament scholar Adele Reinhartz, whom I quoted earlier, draws attention to the way the story of Mary, Martha, and Lazarus does not fit a situation in which Jesus-believers are excluded from the synagogue or socially ostracized from their Jewish neighbors.[22] Rather Mary, Martha, and Lazarus, siblings from the village of Bethany, are all said to be loved by Jesus, a term that elsewhere in the gospel is a synonym for being his disciple. Their neighbors, the Jews, in the story are not separated from them, but come to comfort them, to mourn with them, and appear familiar with Jesus as a figure with healing power. Rather than show one moment of transition to belief in Jesus, the story shows Martha and then Mary coming to deepening Christological understanding in the course of conversation with Jesus. Some believe in Jesus as a result of what they see, and others report Jesus to the Pharisees who begin to plot his death.

Jesus' raising of Lazarus is the final and climactic sign in the series of signs in the gospel—it portrays Jesus as the one who gives life: "What has come into being in him was life" (John 1:3–4). In the interaction of Martha and Mary with each other and with Jesus, the sign also illustrates belief.

The scene opens with an odd and rather extended introduction of the ill man, Lazarus, his two sisters, one of whom is known for an important role later in the story—the one who anointed the Lord with perfume. They send a message to Jesus, "Lord, he whom you love is ill" (John 11:3). Like the mother of Jesus' request at Cana, "they have no wine," the sisters' message is a statement of fact whose request is only implied. Jesus delays. The story points out how strange it is that he loves them yet he does not go quickly to heal his sick friend. In the discussion with the disciples which follows, it is made clear to the reader that Jesus intends to raise the dead, or wake one who has fallen asleep. In the dialogue, the disciples play the role of those with a literal and inadequate understanding of what is happening: "Lord, if he has fallen asleep, he will be all right" (11:12).

When Jesus arrives at Bethany, Lazarus has indeed died; he has been dead for four days. Many of the Jews have come to console Mary and Martha about their brother. As the wedding is a time when families and friends gather in the village with joy, at the time of death friends observe rituals and customs of mourning and consolation. Despite their close association with Jesus, this family is not estranged from its Jewish community. This story may have been related at one time with the story of the raising of Jairus' daughter in Mark 5. There, too, there is a delay in Jesus' arrival, a transition from illness to death, the presence of Jewish mourners. There is a quieter but equally dramatic raising of the child.

Martha goes out to meet Jesus, to intercept him, to lament, to accuse, to express confidence, to argue about theology. In her encounter with Jesus, Martha gives voice to the faith of the Johannine community and utters the belief which is the goal of the gospel.[23] Martha is the figure who represents the faith of the community. Her first words are those of accusation and lament: "Lord, if you had been here, my brother would not have died." She next expresses confidence in Jesus' access to God's power: "But even now I know that God will give you whatever you ask of him." Jesus' next statement is open to misunderstanding: "Your brother will rise again" (John 11:21–23). Yes, she says, he will on the resurrection on the last day. In reply Jesus discloses himself to Martha with the words: "I am the resurrection and the life. Those who believe in me even though they die, will live, and everyone who lives and believes in me will never die. Do you believe this?" (John 11:25–26) Martha confesses belief: "Yes, Lord, I believe that you are the Messiah, the Son of the God, the one coming into the world" (11:27). She represents the community's faith as her words recall the words of the prologue, "The true light, which enlightens everyone, was coming into the world."

Bound to her sister, Martha urges Mary to go to Jesus. She goes along with her friends who have come to console her. When she meets Jesus, she too accuses him using the same words as her sister,

"Lord if you had been here, my brother would not have died." Mary is weeping, doing what mourning people do. So are her friends. And eventually so is Jesus. While I have heard preachers' criticism of this weeping as a sign of lack of faith, the text itself conveys no disapproval of weeping. Just as drinking wine at a wedding is the natural way to celebrate life, weeping is appropriate behavior in response to the death of one you love. It will be echoed later in the story by the weeping of Mary Magdalene at the tomb of Jesus. In response to Mary's lament and the shared distress of the townspeople, Jesus goes to the tomb, instructs the stone to be removed, prays to God and shouts, "Lazarus, come out." "The dead man came out, his hands and feet bound with strips of cloth, and his face wrapped in a cloth. Jesus said to them, 'Unbind him, and let him go'" (11:44). The raising of Lazarus, the final sign in John, like all the signs, is intended to provoke belief. But like the other signs, this most dramatic sign divides those who believe from those who do not. In the story of the gospel, this sign instigates the plot to execute Jesus.

The story of the grief in the Jewish village of Bethany of Martha, Mary, Jesus, and their friends at the death of Lazarus provides an important note of human reality in the schematic picture of good and evil in the gospel. The human reality of sickness and death brings people together, and the finality and loss of death provoke all human beings to ask the ultimate question about what happens after death. Sandra Schneiders writes about this story as a way the later Christian community reflected upon the illness and death of its members in the time after Jesus' resurrection.[24] Reflection on what holds the people in the village together in the face of the death of a sick friend can be a way to begin to read against the grain of the gospel's dualism.

Transforming Conversation at Jacob's Well (John 4:1–42)

Early in the story of the gospel there is a fascinating episode recounting a meeting between Jesus resting by a well and a woman coming to draw water. The conversation which follows, the conclusions reached, and the action motivated by it provide a paradigm or icon for the expansive arc of the gospel and, to a great extent, counteracts the rigidity of its black and white outlook. It is a story of mission and of reconciliation. I treat it here at the physical center of this book, because it represents the leaven, the fresh air, the radical surprise of this gospel.

As I tell the story you will notice that I leave out features that are famous in many retellings: the woman as an outcast, an adulteress, a flirt, of all women most to be pitied. Rather I tell about her as the apostolic hero of John whose vigorous conversation with Jesus illustrates, like Martha's, more and more profound theological insight and offers a vision of spiritual worship and Jesus as the savior of the world. I imagine this story not as a realistic report of an episode during Jesus' lifetime, but a highly structured, developed, version enriched by the experience of the Johannine community with Samaritan mission, women apostolic leaders, and discrimination. Hovering close to the story are shadows of biblical stereotypes, dangerous foreign women, wells as places of marriage proposals, and prophetic denunciations of idolatry as akin to sexual betrayal. These lend drama and humor to the story as they are turned on their heads one by one.

After a somewhat farfetched explanation for Jesus' trip through Samaria, Jesus comes to a site significant in Jewish patriarchal history, Jacob's well. Jesus is there, tired, and we will discover, thirsty. A Samaritan woman comes to do what women do at wells—to draw water. By having a man and woman meet at a well, the story sets up some dramatic expectations—for wells were where couples became engaged. As you read this story, remember that the topics of sex and marriage and of religion always went hand and hand in this world. The relationship between Yahweh and the people of Israel was envisioned as a marriage. Transgression against Yahweh was pictured as adultery or prostitution. Foreign women represented not only dangers of intermarriage, but alliance with foreign gods as well. This is a story that appears to be about romance, but is on another level a story about religious faith.

Jesus asks her for a drink. Readers know that they are alone because the disciples have gone to buy food, another detail which in a realistic narrative would seem contrived. She answers warily, naming the division between a male Jew and Samaritan woman. The editorial comment indicates that the custom of Jews and Samaritans not sharing things may have been unfamiliar to readers. The woman's caution is typical of those who do not occupy a position of power in a relationship. It is the responsibility of the minority to follow the rules of the majority, whose members have the freedom to break the rules. Jesus then launches into a theological/spiritual invitation, using typical Johannine mystery. If anyone is, it is Jesus who offers a seductive invitation: "If you knew the gift of God and who it is that is saying to you, 'Give me a drink,' you would have asked him, and he would have given you living water" (John 4:10). The woman's answer responds to the literal, surface meaning of Jesus' cryptic statement: "Sir, you have no bucket and the well is deep. Where do you get that living water?" (4:11).

Other characters in the narrative employ such literal responses to Jesus. Nicodemus asked, "How can anyone be born after having grown old? Can one enter a second time into the mother's womb and be born?" Philip queried, "Six months wages would not buy enough bread for each of them to get a little" (John 6:7). Her next question expresses curiosity, and at the same time expresses truth of which she is unaware, "Are you greater than our ancestor Jacob, who gave us this well, and with his sons [and daughters] and his flocks drank from it?" (4:12) Jesus replies with another mysterious statement, this time expressed as a proverb or universal statement: "Everyone who drinks of this water will be thirsty again, but those who drink of the water that I will give them will never be thirsty. The water that I will give will become in them a spring of water gushing up to eternal life" (4:13–14). She answers, again asking for the water and expressing its practical value, "so that I may never be thirsty or have to keep coming here to draw water" (4:15).

That Jesus' revelation and the woman's realization of him come through dialogue is an important feature to notice about the Gospel of John. Jesus does no sign here. There is no "miracle." Rather he makes a claim and offers living water to this stranger. To understand it requires back and forth question and answer, partial understanding, correction, and deeper knowledge. Martha's conversation with Jesus after the death of Lazarus is like this too. So are the Easter con-

These dialogues in John's gospel reflect a way individuals and peoples come to faith—through a process of effort and discussion.

versations of Mary and of Thomas. These dialogues in John's gospel reflect a way individuals and peoples come to faith—through a process of effort and discussion. Those who converse with Jesus put Jesus' claims into relationship with their own traditions and beliefs: I know he will be raised on the last day. I know that the Messiah will come. I am the resurrection and the life. I am he, the one who is speaking to you.

For modern readers, Jesus' change of subject to husbands, "go call your husband and come back," appears abrupt. However, the pairing of romance and religion in the biblical imagination—more than one husband and more than one god—helps to make sense of this convention about marriage here. The history of commentary on this story that speculates upon the lurid details of the woman's marital history misses the point. As a Samaritan woman she bears the history of her people who have worshipped five false gods after the Assyrian captivity (2 Kings 17:13–34). This knowledge causes Jesus to question her. This episode of unfaithfulness is an important issue in the dispute and, from the Jewish point of view, the cause of the bad blood between Jews and Samaritans. The other issue is the place of worship, the next topic that the woman raises.

While at the beginning of the story it may have appeared remarkable that Jesus, a male Jew, was asking for a drink from a woman of Samaria, what is remarkable now is the urgency and importance of the content of their discussion. Jesus now speaks of the future. He uses "Woman" to address her as he does with his mother at the wedding in John 2:4 and at the cross in John 19:26. The "hour" refers to the hour of Jesus' death and to the hour of consummation as it does here. At this time both worship on Mount Gerazim and in Jerusalem will be irrelevant, "the hour is coming, and is now here, when true worshippers will worship the Father in spirit and truth" (4:23). Even the distinction between Jew and Samaritan, so important to the interaction of Jesus and the woman here, will no longer pertain when the hour comes.

The extraordinary conversation comes to an end with the woman asserting her knowledge of the coming Messiah and her confidence that he will "proclaim all things to us" (4:25) and Jesus discloses himself in the form of an "I AM" statement: "I am he, the one who is speaking to you" (4:26).

The self-revelation of Jesus to this Samaritan causes her to become an apostle to her own people, a missionary in the city of Sychar. If Jesus' public ministry in the book of signs ends in disappointment and failure, it begins with success in Samaria. This may reflect the historical fact of a mission of the apostles to Samaria after the resurrection.

The narrator tells that when the disciples returned, they were astonished that he was speaking to a woman, but asked no questions about it. This detail may reflect that the role of women as leaders and missionaries in the Johannine community was a source of controversy, a fact that is evidenced in a great deal of early Christian literature. The woman leaves her water jar, goes to the city and testifies to the people, who leave the city and go on their way to him. She is an effective missionary, and her mission follows the pattern of evangelism portrayed by Philip and the others. First the Samaritan people believe because of her testimony, then they go and "stay" with Jesus and hear his word and believe on that basis. Brought to his presence by testimony of others, believers come to a deeper level of belief through their direct experience of Jesus. Now the Samaritan city dwellers proclaim, "we know that this is truly the Savior of the world" (4:42). The title "savior of the world" indicates the universal breadth of Jesus' reach, beyond Jews and Samaritans, to the whole world.

A Samaritan hero in the gospel does not necessarily contradict the general anti-Jewish perspective of the gospel as a whole. The woman of Samaria in the gospel's outlook could be an elevation of the traditional Jewish enemy at the expense of the ruling Jewish authorities, as in Luke's parable of the "good Samaritan." In this perspective, the successful conversion of the Samaritans would contrast with the failure to persuade Jews to belief in Jesus as the Son of God. However, I see in this story energy that when harnessed loosens the potentially potent dualism of the gospel's perspective. The vision of true worshippers worshipping God in spirit and in truth, having gone beyond historical and liturgical disputes, is an ideal to hold on to even in a pluralistic world. The encounter, conversion, and transformation of the woman of Samaria epitomize the way the gospel employs humor and irony to undercut expectations and puncture prejudices. The story sets up expectations for a wedding and fulfills them by incorporating the Samaritans into a new covenant. The woman doesn't get a husband, but instead gets a new job. She indeed doesn't have to keep going to the well to draw water—she abandons her jar by the wayside. The humor in the transmission of gossip about five husbands from the mouth of a "prophet," the woman's utter lack of shame and her boldness in proclamation, her transition from solitude to people-intensive ministry—all these untamable details keep the story open and prevent the simple conclusions about belief and unbelief from being too "simplistic."

> The vision of true worshippers worshipping God in spirit and in truth, having gone beyond historical and liturgical disputes, is an ideal to hold on to even in a pluralistic world.

The language of hate in the Gospel of John is real. Denied, it can do damage to others and to ourselves. Acknowledged, it can be addressed. Understanding the history of the community and of the painful and complex parting of ways between emerging Christianity and rabbinic Judaism at the time of the writing of the gospels helps to interpret the violent and uncompromising language. Opposing the severe dualism of some passages with the gospel's assertion of the Christ's incarnation can prevent denial and denigration of the material world. We can hold up Mary, Martha, and the villagers of Bethany as models of faithful people in the face of grief. We can celebrate the woman of Samaria and the women and men of Sychar and anticipate the hour when true worshippers will worship the Father in spirit and in truth.

Continuing the Conversation . . .

For a personal and scholarly engagement with the Gospel of John, see Adele Reinhartz, *Befriending the Beloved Disciple: A Jewish Reading of the Gospel of John* (New York: Continuum, 2001).

The classic treatment of the relationship of the theological outlook of John and its social setting is Wayne Meeks, "The Man from Heaven in Johannine Sectarianism." *Journal of Biblical Literature* 91 (1972): 44–72.

For a reading of John that emphasizes its sectarian character and missionary dimensions, see David Rensburger, *Johannine Faith and Liberating Community* (Philadelphia: Westminster, 1988).

The formation of rabbinic Judaism and orthodox Christianity is described and analyzed in Alan F. Segal, *Rebecca's Children: Judaism and Christianity in the Roman World* (Cambridge: Harvard University Press, 1986).

CHAPTER FIVE

The Beloved Community: Leadership among the Disciples Whom Jesus Loves

When the hour had come for him to be glorified by you, his heavenly Father, having loved his own who were in the world, he loved them to the end . . .

EUCHARISTIC PRAYER D, BCP 374

Imagine the Last Supper as you know it from other gospels and from paintings in museums. What you expect perhaps is a hurried Passover dinner in an upper room. Jesus takes a loaf of bread, breaks it, and gives it to them: "Take; this is my body." Surrounding him at a standard size table are his twelve male disciples facing the painter or the camera to be recorded for future believers to contemplate (Mark 14:12–25). Now picture this supper askew, with its most familiar element, the institution of the Eucharist, missing, and in its place another rite. Imagine that this rite is followed by hours of teaching, which spin and weave and expand the significance of that rite and reflect back upon the meaning of Jesus' encounters during his encampment in the world.

Is it as though a beloved teacher is about to retire and has one last meal to share with his students? Or it is as through a very ill parent is preparing her family for her death? Most urgent in these hours is to review and to reinforce the teaching covered during the teacher's career. What is crucial as death approaches is to reassure the children of your love, to assure them that you have made provision for them, and to give hope. You want to give them a tangible gift or do something that they will never forget. You want to set an example to carry these students or this family into the future. Who is present at this seminar, this solemn feast? All the followers during the teacher's life are there, and all the former students with their students. All the parent's children and their cousins and their children and companions have assembled. It's crowded.

At this most concentrated moment, when everyone is paying attention, Jesus gets up from the table. We know his thoughts: "Jesus knew that his hour had come to depart from this world and go to the Father." We know what he feels, "Having loved his own who were in the world, he loved them to the end"(John 13:1). He moves deliberately, almost liturgically: "[He] got up from the table, took off his outer robe, and tied a towel around himself. Then he poured water into a basin and began to wash the disciples' feet and to wipe them with the towel that was wrapped around him" (13:4–5). After he has finished he instructs them that as his students they must wash each others' feet: "For I have set you an example, that you also should do as I have done to you" (13:15).

The dinner doesn't end quickly—it goes on late into the night. Jesus teaches one more lesson; like Moses, he announces a law: "I give you a new commandment, that you love one another. Just as I have loved you, you also should love one another. By this everyone will know that you are my disciples, if you have love for one another" (13:34–35).

He then teaches, preaches, promises a gift, and prays over the space of four chapters in John 14–17, which have become some of the most cherished of all Scripture. Those students and followers and family members will take on Jesus' work after he goes where they cannot.

Let's get back to imagining the scene, now with the focus on those present, those hearing this teaching, those he calls his friends. We know for sure that the disciple whom Jesus loved was at this supper, and Judas Iscariot, and Peter, because the text says so. But I think back on the earlier chapters of John. I see the woman of Samaria there, accompanied by some friends from Sychar. I see Philip and Nathanael, perhaps the man from Siloam, the man no longer blind,

Mary and Martha and Lazarus, Thomas, and Mary Magdalene. It's a crowded and colorful dinner, and there's no time for a picture. I see the large company of friends, those whom Jesus loves and calls his disciples finishing dinner, feeling their feet being washed by the kneeling Jesus. They listen carefully and prepare to receive the promised gifts and carry on the work of laying down their lives for one another. The friends of Jesus, those whom Jesus loves, is a broad and wide category, a roomy term with space for many, for any who can attempt to obey Jesus' commandment: "love one another as I have loved you."

The friends of Jesus, those whom Jesus loves, is a broad and wide category, a roomy term, with space for many, for any who can attempt to obey Jesus' commandment: "love one another as I have loved you."

In describing this scene in John, I have exaggerated features of John's account of the Last Supper which are different from that of the other evangelists—that it is not a Passover supper and that it is followed by lengthy discourses of teaching. What is most prominent at the center of the meal, interrupted by episodes of the betrayal, is the washing of feet, a practice unmentioned in other gospels. Jesus speaks of discipleship in a distinctive way—as loving one another, as being friends. Throughout the sequence of signs and dialogues in the first half of the gospel, vividly characterized followers and leaders emerge, again unmentioned in other gospels. The twelve disciples, a numbered group so important in Mark, are mentioned only in John 6:67–71 and 20:24. And the hero of the gospel on whom the tradition rests is an anonymous disciple, mysteriously called the disciple whom Jesus loved. The attendance of these particular leaders and friends, as well as the twelve we imagine from the other gospels, is consistent with the logic of leadership as the author has set it up in this gospel.

This gospel links leadership with love by and for Jesus.

The unconventional picture of the Last Supper serves to introduce the subject of leadership and authority in John's gospel. This gospel links leadership with love by and for Jesus. While this democratic view of leadership is in tension with traditions known to John of the twelve disciples, exclusively male leadership, and the prime role of Peter, it bubbles up in a number of episodes in John and subtly calls into question other notions of authority important in the developing Christian tradition.

To explore this aspect of the Fourth Gospel, I will describe the teaching of Jesus about friendship in the farewell discourse as a model of relationship of mutual care and companionship. I will give close attention to the anointing of Jesus by Mary of Bethany at the dinner which precedes and prefigures the Last Supper. I will show how the beloved disciple appears at key moments in the gospel and serves as a model for readers and future disciples. The gospel's particular understanding of the church supported by the activity of the Paraclete, who is the presence of Jesus in his absence, has far reaching implications for how it views leadership. I will explore the role of the Paraclete and the significance of prophecy and vision in authorizing disciples for ministry and leadership.

I Have Called You Friends—Being a Disciple

I do not call you servants any longer, because the servant does not know what the master is doing; but I have called you friends . . .

(JOHN 15:15)

The Gospel of John understands Jesus' ministry, his coming to "tent" among us, and his relationship with his disciples throughout subsequent generations as friendship. The language of friendship includes the word for "to love," *phileo*, the word for friend, *philos*, and the synonym for *phileo*, *agapao*. Friendship has deep resonances in the cultural world of the Fourth Gospel in the writings of the Greco-Roman philosophers and in the Jewish writings of the Hellenistic world. Friendship was a virtue characterized by mutual respect and good will. Somewhat like our modern ideals of friendship, the relationship between friends involved day-to-day companionship and assistance in crisis. Friends took risks for one another and endured suffering together.[25] A more familiar way of talking about this language of friendship might be "love." Love is indeed a theme of John, but understanding the love language as part of the cultural conventions of friendship highlights the fact that "love" is not a term belonging to technical religious vocabulary, as we have come to know it, but is connected with the language and valued relationships of everyday life. Friendship in the world of John is not a more informal or less significant term than love—it is all the more important.

"No one has greater love than this, to lay down one's life for one's friends" (John 15:13). Jesus' death is an exercise of love, the putting down of his life, like the washing of feet. Jesus' exaltation to the Father and his preparation of a dwelling for those he loves is an expression of friendship. Disciples of Jesus in John are Jesus' friends. This group is intimate, but not elite. The gospel speaks of no special title or office, not apostle or deacon or elder, other than *philos*, friend.

The farewell discourse teaches that Jesus' love for the disciples mandates their love for each other: "love one another as I have loved you." Through Jesus' love for them, they are drawn into God's love:

> The hour is coming when I will no longer speak to you in figures, but will tell you plainly of the Father. On that day you will ask in my name. I do not say to you that I will ask the Father on your behalf; for the Father himself loves you, because you have loved me and have believed that I came from God. (John 16:25–27)

By Jesus' example he makes his friends to be friends of God. In Hellenistic Greek writings, Abraham and Moses are called "friend of God." Like Wisdom "in every generation . . . passes into holy souls and makes them friends of God" (Wis 7:27), Jesus creates a community of friends.

Explicit language of love and friendship increases in the second half of the gospel, what Raymond Brown has called "the Book of Glory," after Jesus' public ministry is over and when he turns to address his teaching to the community of the beloved disciples. If you listen carefully to the tone of Jesus' teaching, you might hear the shift in Jesus' speech to more intimacy and less hostility, more the gospel of love and less the gospel of hate.

Students in my classes have observed this shift; some have even said that Jesus seems like a different character in the Book of Glory. It is intriguing to reflect on the meaning of this division in the gospel. The structure of Mark's gospel, too, appears divided between Mark 1–8:21, which narrate Jesus' deeds of power, and then Mark 8:22–10:52, a section structured around teaching to the disciples about his passion and death and how to be disciples. Could it be that the public ministry material includes more controversy and argument while the "private" teaching is remembered more warmly? In Mark's gospel during the teaching about discipleship, one incident occurs to show the disciples in a negative light—James and John's request of Jesus, "Grant us to sit, one at your right hand and one at your left in your glory." During the discourses in John, the disciples mainly listen. Could it be that the author of John is less critical of the broad group of those whom Jesus loves, the ancestors of John's own community, than Mark is of the named disciples? It may be that in addressing insiders, Jesus' tone is more protective and less combative. Or it may be that the discourses of the Risen Christ are more thoroughly colored by the reassuring tenor of the post-Easter Jesus.

Motifs of friendship and love, however, are not restricted to the second part of the gospel. The imagined picture of the Last Supper in which figures important in the public ministry are present at the table during the private teaching brings together these two parts of the gospel. The prologue's affirmation that the word became flesh and tented among us is an image of accompaniment and companionship typical of friendship. The extended conversations with Philip and Nathanael, with Nicodemus, the woman at the well, the man at the pool, and the man born blind express friendship. Friends share weddings, picnics, and celebratory dinners. The ideal of accompaniment is wonderfully woven through the gospel in the modest word *meno*, to remain. The same verb is translated as "to stay," "to remain," "to dwell," "to abide." It can mean "stay" as in "where are you staying?" (1:38–39). The Samaritans ask Jesus to stay with them and he complies (4:40). The word also refers to Jesus' presence with them during his lifetime, "I have said these things to you while I am still with you" (literally, while I am staying with you) (14:25). Translated as "abide," the verb describes the mutual indwelling of the God, Jesus, and the disciples whom he loves: "As the Father has loved me, so I have loved you; abide in my love. If you keep my commandments, you will abide in my love, just as I have kept my Father's commandments and abide in his love" (John 15:9–10). Whenever it appears, the verb *meno* evokes the Johannine sense of divine presence and companionship.

Mary Anoints Jesus at Bethany—
The Second-to-Last Supper

One way of thinking about the structure of the Gospel of John is as a series of feasts, beginning with the wedding and continuing with the picnic in the wilderness. Nearer the time of Jesus' leave-taking, two dinners take place, a dinner at Bethany and a dinner at Jerusalem. In the final episode of the gospel, after it has ended once, Jesus appears again for a breakfast of bread and fish with Peter and the disciples. This gospel pictures intimacy and friendship as feasting with Jesus. These ordinary meals are revelatory. To continue to explore the idea of leadership in John, I want to give particular attention to one of these dinners, the dinner at Bethany in John 12:1–8 and its important parallels with the washing of feet dinner in John 13:1–17. The two meals reflect one another, as though mirror images. Both are suppers; both involve the actions of washing and wiping, interpreted as acts of love and self-sacrifice. At both are gathered those whom Jesus loves. At each, impending death impinges on the celebration. Judas, the villain, is present. It is at the home of Mary and Martha. Martha is said to serve. The host is Mary.

Now, the memorable action of this dinner is the anointing of Jesus by Mary. Because there are so many variations of the story of Jesus being anointed by a woman in the gospels and the stories bear family resemblances to one another, it is easy to get the stories mixed up. If one hears these stories all at once, it is harder to distinguish the special role of Mary here in this scene in John's gospel. She is the host, not the uninvited intruder as in some versions of the story (Luke 7:36–50). As in Mark 14:3–9, her act is a critical recognition of Jesus, but unlike that story, she has a name, and it's a very important name in John's community. The community of the beloved disciple, whose traditions are written by John, cared that the woman who recognized Jesus before his passion be remembered not only with a name, but with an important name, that she be remembered as one of the significant disciples among those who established the community: Mary, sister of Martha, sister of Lazarus, the family whom Jesus loved. The text links this story to the story of the raising of Mary and Martha's brother in John 11: "Now a certain man was ill, Lazarus of Bethany, the village of Mary and her sister Martha. Mary was the one who anointed the Lord with perfume and wiped his feet with her hair; her brother Lazarus was ill" (John 11:1–2).

Mary personified grief and love in the episode before, when she weeps at her brother's death and entreats, "Lord if you had been here my brother would not have died." She weeps and Jesus weeps. The family partakes of this dinner in the wake of one grief and in the darkening shadow of another. Mary prepares to lose Jesus. She takes the perfume, anoints Jesus' feet, wipes them with her hair. The house was filled with the fragrance of the perfume.

The Christians of the Fourth Gospel not only told what she did in memory of her, as directed in Mark's version, but they incorporated her act into the liturgical memory of the community. The details, the supper, the serving, the wiping, Judas, all parallel the Last Supper, and show how this community interpreted the anointing by Mary. She anticipated and enacted what Jesus was to command a few nights later. Mary, as one whom Jesus loved, did what the friends were taught to do by Jesus. It is the second-to-last supper, and Mary plays the role of Jesus, kneeling, wiping, pouring out substance of inestimable value. Mary is the host, the one who knows what is to come, the one who anticipates Jesus' example of foot-washing and symbolically washes him.

It is unfortunate that during the history of interpretation, this story has become so muddled with the woman from the city who was a sinner in Luke 7:36–50 and the busy and lazy sisters, Mary and Martha, in Luke 10:38–42. When read in its place in the Gospel of John, the story eloquently proclaims Mary's authority and leadership in the memory of this community.

Who is the Beloved Disciple?

The character of the disciple whom Jesus loved, to whom many give the name the beloved disciple, is an intriguing figure to think about as we explore leadership in this gospel. The figure entered prominently into the topic of the gospel's authorship in chapter 1. At the end of the second "ending" of the gospel, as part of the conversation between Peter and Jesus, the narrator refers to a rumor that the beloved disciple would not die. Then the narrator clarifies this rumor as a misunderstanding and identifies the beloved disciple as the one who is passing on the tradition to the evangelist. The Johannine community traced its traditions to this figure.

A similar reference to this disciple's testimony comes in John 19:35 at the time when blood and water flow from Jesus' side, "He who saw this has testified so that you also may believe. His testimony is true, and he knows that he tells the truth." The character appears in the gospel first at the Last Supper when a disciple whom Jesus loved is described as "reclining next to him," (John 13:23) or, more literally, leaning on Jesus' chest. The King James translation renders it "leaning on Jesus' bosom." This pose embodies intimacy and close relationship. The word *kolpos*, "chest," "heart," or "bosom," is featured in the prologue of the gospel in John 1:18: "It is God the only Son, who is close to the Father's heart, who has made him known." These two uses of the word suggest a parallel between the beloved disciple's intimate relationship with Jesus and the relationship of the Father and Son.

In addition to the role of witness and transmitter of tradition, the disciple whom Jesus loves will function as a member of Jesus' family after his death. The narrator tells of Jesus' words from the cross: "When Jesus saw his mother and the disciple whom he loved standing beside her, he said to his mother, "Woman, here is your son." Then he said to the disciple, "Here is your mother." And from that hour the disciple took her into his own home" (John 19:26–27).

With these words Jesus establishes a new kindred relationship between his own mother and the disciple. Jesus births a symbolic new family to continue after his return to the Father. All disciples of Jesus can call God their Father, as Mary Magdalene can in 20:17 call Jesus' mother their own mother, and call each other brothers and sisters.

The "disciple whom Jesus loved" has a privileged role in the story. This disciple is also present at the empty tomb, arrives after Peter, enters after him, and is said to "believe." Here and at the supper, he appears to be of superior importance to Peter, the disciple whom Luke and Matthew portray as preeminent. The beloved disciple, perhaps the founder of this community, is the personal link between the community and the traditions of Jesus.

The presence of the beloved disciple in the gospel shows that leadership in John is related not to a specific appointment—"on this rock I will build my church" (Matt 16:18)—or presence on the mountain of transfiguration, but primarily upon the relationship of love, or of friendship, with Jesus. Leadership is also linked with seeing and with witnessing. The beloved disciple shares this relationship with all the other disciples of Jesus who have received the commandment, "love one another as I have loved you." The disciple whom Jesus loved is both special and privileged, *and* stands for all the disciples. This person is never called "the disciple whom Jesus loved best" but simply the disciple whom Jesus loved. I have chosen not to capitalize the term "the beloved disciple" as a proper name in order to underscore this figure's representative character.

The disciple whom Jesus loved is both special and privileged, and stands for all the disciples.

The anonymity of this person—the fact that he or she does not have a name—is very important. Although there are hints in the text that other characters may be this disciple: Mary of Bethany, Martha, Lazarus, Thomas, Mary Magdalene, the gospel never gives a name. Scholars have written volumes arguing for one or another candidate for this person with no satisfactory resolution.[26] The namelessness of this figure means that anyone in the story might be this person and that any reader of the gospel might identify with the one Jesus loved. The figure's anonymity even leaves ambiguous whether this disciple is male or female. The women, Mary and Martha of Bethany and Mary Magdalene, qualify to be the disciple whom Jesus loved. Mary and Martha are both spoken of as being loved by Jesus and communicate their faith in him. Mary Magdalene hears and sees Jesus outside the tomb and he speaks her name. The figure's namelessness attracts names to it, yet always resists strict identification.

Another Advocate to Be with You Forever

O Comforter, draw near, within my heart appear, and kindle it thy holy flame bestowing.

BIANCO DE SIENA; TR. RICHARD FREDERICK LITTLEDALE, HYMNAL 1982, 516

Jesus teaches those he loves how they will continue as a community of his friends after he has returned to the Father, when he has gone where they cannot come. As a retiring teacher or as a parent saying goodbye for the last time, Jesus promises them a gift:

If you love me, you will keep my commandments. And I will ask the Father, and he will give you another Advocate, to be with you forever. This is the Spirit of truth, whom the world cannot receive, because it neither sees him nor knows him. You know him, because he abides with you, and he will be in you. (John 14:15–17)

The word translated as Advocate is the Greek word, *paracletos*, a word that occurs only in John (14:16, 14:26, 15:26; 16:7). Also called in John "the Spirit of Truth," the Paraclete resembles what the other gospels calls the Holy Spirit, but it has its own distinctive functions and role in John's understanding of Christ and the church. When "Paraclete" is translated as counselor or comforter, the pastoral and reassuring dimensions of its role are highlighted. "Advocate" connotes one who testifies, defends, and supports the community as Jesus has. The legal connotations of Advocate are significant—there is an implied trial setting in which witnesses are called to testify on behalf of those on trial.[27] Jesus has been the first Advocate, and he promises the other Advocate will come after his death to act as teacher in the community. The presence of the Paraclete alleviates the problem of leadership succession after the absence of Mary, Martha, Peter, and the beloved disciple. For that Advocate will lead and guide the community into the future. The gift of the Paraclete addresses these questions and those that might be asked by successive generations of the Johannine community of friends:

- Who will be with us?
- Who will take care of us as Father and Mother?
- How will the traditions be passed down and taught?
- Who will teach us and remind us?
- Who will give us peace?
- Who will testify to Jesus?
- Who will advocate for us in a hostile world?
- Who will tell us what to do/how to be now?
- Who will speak?

Just as the friends know Jesus, so they know the Paraclete (John 14:17) and he "abides with them, and will be in or among them." The Paraclete will also "teach you everything, and remind you of all that I have said to you" (14:26). The vital and active presence of the

Paraclete will keep on teaching in continuity with Jesus' teaching and will remind them what Jesus said. The presence of the Paraclete ensures that the community will continue to "hear" Jesus' words and that Jesus will continue to "speak." The community's belief in the presence of the Paraclete may have led to the generation of discourses and sayings within the Johannine community. The Spirit of Truth may help to explain the distinctive traditions known to the Johannine community and unknown in synoptic tradition: "I still have many things to say to you, but you cannot bear them now. When the Spirit of truth comes, he will guide you into all the truth; for he will not speak on his own, but will speak whatever he hears, and he will declare to you the things that are to come" (John 16:12–14).

Jesus has not finished speaking in the community. The abiding Paraclete promises more to come. The expectation that prophetic experience is to continue may account for the open-endedness at the end of the gospel. Ongoing teaching and speaking might not be controlled or contained in books alone: "But there are also many other things that Jesus did; if every one of them were written down, I suppose that the world itself could not contain the books that would be written" (John 21:25).

For the Gospel of John, leadership in the community flows out of being a friend of Jesus. Being Jesus' friend requires allowing Jesus to wash your feet and to wash the feet of your friends in Christ. Such service creates a relationship not of master and slave, but of friend and friend. "Love one another as I have loved you" is the Johannine Jesus' summary of the law, the new commandment. In its history this community of friends has known particular leaders who represent apostleship (the woman of Samaria), confession of faith (Martha of Bethany), and Christ-like service and love (Mary of Bethany). The group of disciples extends far beyond any twelve individuals. The disciple around whom the memory of the community centers is not Peter or James or John, but an unnamed figure, his or her epithet describing Jesus' love. This figure leans on Jesus' bosom. This person receives a new mother at the time of Jesus' death and watches Jesus' wound flow blood and water. At the tomb the disciple sees and believes. And yet this person remains nameless. He is no particular disciple. She is every disciple.

After the departure of Jesus and the death of all the founding figures and models of the community, the sisters and brothers in the church are not orphaned children or defendants without representation. The Paraclete is Jesus' representative, the one who abides in and among them, or as the Book of Common Prayer (336, 337) puts it, "that he may dwell in us and we in him."

Prophecy and Vision Authorize Leaders

The Johannine community who authored this gospel experienced the vigorous activity of the Paraclete in their midst. The Advocate's teaching, reminding, and speaking kept their community hopeful and joyful and creative in the generations after Jesus' exaltation and after their founding members had died. The gospel emphasizes that it is a vision of Jesus that evokes belief and authorizes leadership. Letters of Paul show that receiving a vision of the risen Lord called Paul to apostleship. Appearances of Jesus changed the lives of many, many followers after the resurrection.

> For I handed on to you as of first importance what I in turn had received: that Christ died for our sins in accordance with the scriptures, and that he was buried, and that he was raised on the third day in accordance with the scriptures, and that he appeared to Cephas, then to the twelve. Then he appeared to more than five hundred brothers and sisters at one time, most of whom are still alive, though some have died. Then he appeared to James, then to all the apostles. (1 Cor 15:3–7)

In John the act of seeing is emphasized over and over again as the medium through which people come to belief. The speaker of the prologue affirms, "we have seen his glory." Jesus promises Nathanael that "you will see greater things than these." On one level this seeing simply refers to the characters in the story being present to see Jesus do his signs. On another, this seeing is the mystical experience of seeing or spiritual insight which those who have not participated in Jesus' ministry during his lifetime may have.

Like the Paraclete, and like the authority of the beloved disciple, the book functions as a way to call to mind or symbolize Jesus' presence.

Seeing Jesus is good, and the gospel itself functions to create vision and sight, so that readers can indeed "see." The signs are written so that readers can see and hear and believe. Like the Paraclete, and like the authority of the beloved disciple, the book functions as a way to call to mind or symbolize Jesus' presence.

John's gospel describes discipleship as friendship, a model of mutuality in contrast with mastery and slavery. Leadership within this community is represented by faithful women who work as apostles and spokespersons for the faith of the Johannine community. Mary of Bethany performs Christ-like washing of Jesus' own feet. The role of leadership for every person among the friends is suggested by the nameless beloved disciple. The activity of the Paraclete as Counselor and Advocate ensures that the community neither forgets nor becomes rigid. Those who watch and listen will see and hear Jesus.

Continuing the Conversation . . .

For a full treatment of the friendship motif in John, see Sharon Ringe, *Wisdom's Friends: Community and Christology in the Fourth Gospel* (Louisville: Westminster John Knox Press, 1999).

For further reading on the beloved disciple, see Alan Culpepper, *John, the Son of Zebedee: The Life of a Legend* (Columbia: University of South Carolina Press, 1994).

For an introduction to feminist scholarship on John, see Amy Jill Levine, ed. with Marianne Blickenstaff, *A Feminist Companion to John* (New York: Sheffield, 2003).

CHAPTER SIX

Multiple Modes of Knowing: Easter in John

Jesus said to her, "Mary!" She turned and said to him in Hebrew, "Rabbouni!" (which means Teacher).

(JOHN 20:16)

O God, whose Son Jesus is the good shepherd of your people: Grant that when we hear his voice we may know him who calls us each by name, and follow where he leads; who, with you and the Holy Spirit, lives and reigns, one God, for ever and ever. Amen

(BCP, 225)

John's gospel invites readers to believe. The gospel itself does what the disciple whom Jesus loved does—it testifies to Jesus. The way this gospel testifies is as important as what it says; the medium, the form of communication, is the message. And the message can only be properly spoken through the complex, intricate, and playful style of John. We have seen some of John's ways in the stories we have read closely. First we noticed the first ending of the gospel which was ignored but not eliminated, and the two voices in the prologue inter-spliced together. The text preserves marks of its own past as it narrates history. We saw how the signs of the wedding and the picnic reported events whose meanings ran deep, yet whose significance depended upon the good wine and true bread. We followed the form of dialogue between Jesus and the woman of Samaria and Martha and Mary in which those conversing with Jesus are brought from the literal to the symbolic, from the traditional creed to the novel belief, from caution to embrace. And these dialogues do not go in a straight line, but meander and set up expectations that are overturned. Anointing and foot washing mirror one another. The unnamed disciple entices readers to affix a name, but with no success. The style of John does not decorate the meaning but embodies it. The paradox and mystery and elusiveness of the Word coming into the world can be expressed in no other way.

In this final chapter I want to explore a feature of the gospel that I called in the introduction "patient and generous." It is the way the gospel offers repeated and varied invitations or occasions to believe. Jesus does sign after sign, each showing his glory but each unique. He preaches on and on, choosing paradigms, bread, light, shepherd. He performs the washing of feet. As much as each episode is unique, when you open any page

The way this gospel testifies is as important as what it says; the medium, the form of communication, is the message.

of John, you recognize the theological outlook and the distinctive language. The repetitiveness of John is the message too. Not only are there lots of signs Jesus did, but it takes lots of signs to come near to realizing the purpose of the gospel—the calling forth of belief.

The gospel employs repetition and variation not only in the signs and discourses, but in the climax of the gospel: the stories of Easter. This chapter will look at how John tells the stories of Easter—the empty tomb and the appearances of the Risen Christ. We will recognize in these stories the interplay of literal and symbolic, the revelatory dialogue, the irony, and the surprise which we have seen in the other scenes in the gospel. We will see the themes of authority, vision, and intimacy play together. The sequence of appearances to those Jesus loved show him offering to people the means to understand and to believe.

Jesus' Friends See Jesus after Easter

John, like all the gospels, is written in the light of Easter. That is, the community who tells of Jesus' teaching and deeds of power know Christ alive among them and know his presence in their worship and their reading of Scripture. When God raised Jesus, God vindicated him and gave hope to his suffering friends. The letters and gospels in the New Testament speak of the explosive experience of the resurrection among the communities of Jesus' followers. They experienced the resurrection when the living Jesus appeared to them, reassured them, read the Scriptures, broke bread. They were galvanized and energized for their own ministry of teaching and healing. Those who saw Jesus were authorized or commissioned for ministry, service, and evangelism. Paul writes of his experience of Jesus' appearance in the text from 1 Corinthians 15:3–7 quoted in chapter 5.

They experienced the resurrection when the living Jesus appeared to them, reassured them, read the Scriptures, broke bread.

We know that there were many stories of Jesus' appearances because the gospels preserve a number of them, but in no two gospels are they identical. In Matthew, Jesus appears to Mary Magdalene and the other Mary outside the tomb, greets them, tells them not to be afraid, and commissions them to tell the others. He appears to the eleven disciples on the mountain and orders them to make disciples, baptize, and teach. In Luke, Jesus walks with two disciples on their way to Emmaus and then shows the disciples his hands and feet and eats fish in their presence. Mark tells of no appearances but ends with the vision of the empty tomb to Mary Magdalene, Mary, the mother of James, and Salome. An ending later added to Mark reports an appearance to Mary Magdalene, to two disciples, and then to the eleven. The Gospel of John relates four appearances—one to Mary Magdalene, one to the disciples without Thomas, one to Thomas and the rest, and in the epilogue, one to a group of disciples including the disciple whom Jesus loved and Peter. It is clear that the series of scenes between Jesus and his friends at Easter in John share John's literary and theological perspective. They speak of leadership, vision, community, belief, and ministry.

What Mary Magdalene Sees and Hears

The Easter story in John draws together the themes of seeking, seeing, conversing, and believing so meaningful in the gospel and weaves them into the series of meetings between Jesus and his friends. Although it resembles the stories of Easter in the other gospels, the scene in John is most fruitfully understood in the context of the Fourth Gospel's own sensibility and style.

Only in John is Jesus buried in a garden. The garden summons up the garden of Eden in the story of creation. It also recalls the garden central in the Song of Songs where the lovers meet and woo. The motif of the lover seeking his or her beloved hums underneath this story, much as the engagement and wedding theme coexisted with the theological conversation in the story of the woman of Samaria. By now we have seen how this gospel conceives of relationship with Jesus and with God in the language of love and friendship.

In the opening story of Easter morning, John shows each person, Mary Magdalene, the disciple whom Jesus loved, and Simon Peter, seeing and drawing conclusions on the basis of what they see. It is not perfectly clear what or how complete is the belief of those who enter the tomb, but it is clear that this story includes all three characters to different extents in this experience of Easter.

John tells of only one person, Mary Magdalene, coming to the tomb. Like the woman of Samaria, Martha, and Thomas, Mary Magdalene is a representative character. John focuses attention on the individual woman's meeting with Jesus. John's story does not imply that Mary is a possessed woman, a sinner, or a prostitute. Here she is the same Mary Magdalene who stood at the cross with Jesus' mother and the other women. In my experience, it is hard for many modern readers to let go of the image of Mary, the repentant and reformed sinner, coming in the dark to the tomb on the first day of the week. But as one grows more acquainted with the perspectives of the Fourth Gospel, one sees that the nuances of meaning in the conversation between Jesus and Mary are not illuminated by the idea, which is foreign to John and to the synoptic gospels, of Mary as a prostitute.

When she comes Mary sees that the stone is gone. We know that she concludes that "they have taken the Lord out of the tomb, and we do not know where they have laid him" (John 20:2) because those are her words to Simon Peter and the other disciple when she runs to tell them. Her statement exemplifies Johannine misunderstanding, in which there is some truth, but incomplete truth. Jesus *has* been "taken" from the tomb. Her words set up the question that has occurred throughout the gospel, "where is Jesus?" In the first chapter Jesus asked two disciples, "what are you looking for?" and they said, "Rabbi (which translated means Teacher), where are you staying?"

(1:35–38). Peter asks in 13:36, "Lord, where are you going?" The subject of Jesus' farewell discourse is his presence and his absence, in other words, his whereabouts. The scene with Mary concludes with Jesus answering the question, "where?"

The running race between Peter and the other disciple may be a way to portray competition between two important figures who may have been rivals for the loyalty of the Johannine community in its later history. The other disciple arrives first, looks in and sees the grave clothes, "the linen wrappings." Simon Peter then enters, sees"the linen wrappings lying there, and the cloth that had been on Jesus' head, not lying with the linen wrappings but rolled up in a place by itself" (John 20:6–7).

Seeing the more elaborately described grave clothes is clearly important, but the text does not say what or if Peter believes. Peter has been portrayed as misunderstanding Jesus, not allowing him to wash his feet, so it may be that the text implies that he did not believe. The other disciple enters and is said to have seen and believed. He believed on the basis of the sign he saw within the tomb, the burial wrappings and the cloth that had been on Jesus' head.[28]

Mary stands weeping outside the tomb. We know from the story of the illness and death of Lazarus that weeping is a human response to grief, shared by Jesus for those he loves. The text here shows no criticism of Mary's weeping, but the question of both the angels and of Jesus, "why are you weeping?" shows only compassionate inquiry. To the angels' query, Mary repeats her complaint and her ignorance, "they have taken away my Lord, and I do not know where they have laid him" (John 20:13).

The interaction between Mary and Jesus during his appearance to her shares some of the qualities of the dialogue at the well with the woman of Samaria. It appears at first to be a meeting of strangers. Misunderstanding is uncovered through conversation, and lack of recognition shifts to insight. In Mary's physical posture of turning around and her words of dawning knowledge, she conveys coming to belief. After she speaks to the angels, she turns and sees Jesus standing there, "but she did not know that it was Jesus" (John 20:14).

The same motif of Jesus in the guise of a stranger works in Luke in the road to Emmaus story. Jesus repeats the question of the angels,

"Woman, why are you weeping? Whom are you looking for?" (John 20:15). Again as in the opening and at his arrest, Jesus asks who and what people seek. The text tells that Mary thought Jesus to be the gardener, an unrealistic but marvelously ironic mistake. If the garden is Eden, then the gardener would be God. She asks him to tell her *where* he has laid him, so she can take him away. Immediately after the moment of most extreme incorrect understanding, comes the instant of communication and communion. Jesus says her name, "Mary" and she, again turning, speaks one of his names, "Rabbouni." Hearing her own name causes her to recognize Jesus and to respond with his. Like the sheep who recognize the voice of their shepherd, Mary knows Jesus' voice.

Like the sheep who recognize the voice of their shepherd, Mary knows Jesus' voice.

The next part of the conversation is hard to understand, and one popular interpretation is that Jesus is rebuking Mary, forbidding her to touch him. Her wanting to touch him has been said to be a reflection of Mary's overly focused interest on his physical body or her desire to have him and to prevent him from his necessary ascension. However, a more sensible reading is that it is the glorified Jesus that Mary sees in the garden. His instructions to her are not to focus on him, the individual Jesus, literally: "do not hold onto me," (John 20:17) because he has already ascended, but rather to find his presence among his sisters and brothers in the community. Here Jesus uses for the first time the term "sisters and brothers" (the word *adelphoi* includes both male and female siblings) to describe his disciples or his friends, the new family that his death has created, as he instituted the kinship between the disciple and his mother at the cross.[29] When he tells her not to hold on to *me,* Jesus is not criticizing her, but reminding her that his work on earth is accomplished, and that her responsibility is to her family.

Jesus commissions Mary to tell them, "I am ascending to my Father and to your Father, to my God and your God" (John 20:17). These words of Jesus allude to the promise of Ruth to Naomi, that your people shall be my people and your God my God, and they evoke the relationship of friendship between Ruth and her mother-in-law. Mary Magdalene responds to her commission by announcing her vision to the disciples, "I have seen the Lord" (20:18). Her vision incorporates her knowledge that the one she saw is indeed the Lord. It is this announcement that earns Mary the title "the apostle to the apostles." Christ appears to her and she reports her seeing, her vision, to others. In this first of Jesus' appearances in John, he inquires as to the cause of her grief, then reveals himself to her in the speaking of her name. He redirects her attention from his own person to his ongoing presence in the community of his and her brothers and sisters. She obeys and announces her vision and reports his teaching.

Mary's apostolic role in this story in John has led some to argue for her as the character upon whose testimony the gospel is based, the one to whose memory the community depended for its connection with the story of Jesus' ministry, passion, and crucifixion. The prominence of her role here as apostle to the apostles has some important similarities to the place of Mary Magdalene in some of the non-canonical gospels. In both she has visions, spreads the news of her vision to others, and reports what Jesus says to her. On the basis of all the literature about Mary Magdalene in early Christianity, New Testament scholar Jane Schaberg has reconstructed a portrait of Mary as visionary leader and successor to Jesus.[30] Karen King and Elaine Pagels have traced the way that while canonical gospels assert the primacy of Peter and the male disciples of Jesus, the gospels of other early Christians raise up Mary Magdalene as the chief authoritative figure.[31]

He redirects her attention from his own person to his ongoing presence in the community of his and her brothers and sisters.

One of the issues of dispute among early Christian groups seems to have been the legitimacy of women's leadership. The expansive reading of John that I have undertaken here has shown the importance of women as corporate or representative figures in this gospel and has attended to the extraordinary first appearance of Jesus to Mary. Taken with the breadth of the category of friend of Jesus or those whom Jesus loves, the role of women in John's gospel leads me to see that John maintains an openness to leadership that is far broader than Peter and the twelve disciples. The role of the unnamed disciple whom Jesus loves, whether or not one wishes to argue that she is Mary Magdalene, resists restriction of the authority to men.

The Gospel of John complicates the opposition between canonical and non-canonical gospels on the issues of the importance of Mary Magdalene and of the leadership of women in the community.

Appearance at Evening

Breathe on me, Breath of God, fill me with live anew, that I may love what thou dost love, and do what thou wouldst do.

EDWIN HATCH (1835–1889), HYMNAL 1982, 508

The gospel narrates another appearance of Jesus during the evening of that day. If one assumes that the disciples are a completely different group than Mary, Martha, Mary of Bethany, and the other women, then this group would include only the ten male disciples—the twelve minus Judas and without Thomas. If you read "disciples" inclusively and broadly as suggested by the Johannine perspective, then this group would not necessarily be just these ten. The Gospel of Luke, for example, is much more definitive than John about the difference between the group of women followers and the "apostles." In this appearance as in the previous one, Jesus appears mysteriously and is recognized after he speaks and is seen, when he shows his hands and his side. The image of the doors locked from fear contrasts with Jesus' effortless entry. Jesus' words to his friends are the same that he used in his going away instructions, "Peace." His words there are echoed in his greeting here:

> Peace I leave with you; my peace I give to you. I do not give to you as the world gives. Do not let your hearts be troubled, and do not let them be afraid. You heard me say to you, 'I am going away, and I am coming to you.' If you loved me, you would rejoice that I am going to the Father, because the Father is greater than I. (John 14:27–28)

The disciples here do rejoice as Jesus anticipated they would. He repeats the words of peace and then commissions them as well. He breathes on them as God breathed the breath of life into the human being in the garden (Gen 2:7). He gives the Holy Spirit and links it with the ability to forgive and retain others' sins. This moment has some parallels with other scenes in the synoptic gospels, but as we have seen over and over, it has its unique Johannine angle. Unlike the Lukan story of the giving of the Spirit at Pentecost, this is a quiet affair, emphasizing soft wind and not fire (Acts 2:1–13). Unlike the commissioning of Peter as the head of the church in Matthew 16:17–18, here the power to "bind and loose" is given to all the gathered disciples. Because there is no separate event of ascension in John— Jesus' being lifted up on the cross is his exaltation, the equivalent of ascension—the glorified Jesus

> He breathes on them as God breathed the breath of life into the human being in the garden. (Gen 2:7)

simply appears and gives the promised Spirit. Here Jesus gives the disciples what they need to "see" him as Lord, the phrase used to indicate recognition and belief; he speaks peace and shows his hands and side.

What Does Thomas See?

Thomas the Twin missed the Easter evening visit from Jesus. The apostles, like Mary, tell him, "We have seen the Lord." Their testimony is supposed to be enough, just as Mary's would have been enough for the disciples who were not outside the tomb as she had been. But Thomas gives them an obstinate challenge, "unless I see the mark of the nails in his hands, and put my finger in the mark of the nails, and my hand in his side, I will not believe" (John 20:25). The repetitive detail about seeing the mark and the physical exploration of the wounds in hands and side emphasizes the graphic extent of the experience Thomas is demanding. Thomas' defiant claim that he will not believe makes the characterization of him as "doubting Thomas" appear quite mild and feeble. "Doubting" connotes being unsure. The synonym for "not believing" is not "doubting." The Greek word Jesus uses, *apistos*, which English translations render as "doubt," is better translated as "do not be unbelieving." A better name for Thomas might be Demanding Thomas, Defiant Thomas, Spiritually Ambitious Thomas. What Thomas wants is firsthand experience of Jesus' presence, and he describes that experience as both visual and tactile. If Thomas, like Mary, represents a kind of relationship to belief, then he represents one who wants immediacy, physical closeness to the risen Jesus just as the disciple whom Jesus loved was physically close to him.

Jesus' remarkable response to Thomas underlines the point that I am making in this chapter. A week later Jesus appears again through shut doors, offers the greeting of peace, and speaks to Thomas. He offers to Thomas precisely what Thomas had audaciously asked for: "Put your finger here and see my hands. Reach out your hand and put it in my side. Do not doubt but believe" (John 20:27). Literally: "do not be unbelieving but believing." In other words, Jesus tries again. Jesus offers the experience Thomas needs to believe. For Thomas does believe, as we know from his exclamation, "My Lord, and my God."

While much of interpretation throughout history has heartily criticized Thomas, the text gives no hint of censure. Rather, Jesus sets the example of generosity by his gracious offer to see and touch. One point of controversy in the tradition of interpretation is the issue of whether or not Thomas accepted Jesus' offer to put his finger in his wound and his hand in his side. Much commentary and visual art insist that he did not. Perhaps they do so to be consistent with their interpretation of Jesus' instructions to Mary not to hold onto him. Perhaps it is because of reluctance on the part of commentators to imagine human physical contact with the risen Jesus. The text is silent. Perhaps Thomas believed as soon as Jesus made the invitation, and did not need to accept the offer. Perhaps Thomas did indeed see and touch Jesus' wounds as he had so desired. The reader can decide which interpretation best fits the Johannine view of spirit and matter, or one can simply leave it, as the text does, unanswered.

Jesus' final words in John 20:29, "Have you believed because you have seen me? Blessed are those who have not seen and yet have come to believe," have often been read as a criticism of Thomas' need to see. Rather than being addressed to Thomas, Jesus' words are addressed to those readers who come after who will not have Thomas' particular experience of "sight" and yet will come to believe. The next verses directly relate the purpose of writing the signs to engendering or strengthening belief, and imply that this book will aid those who did not see the signs in the presence of the disciples. The use of the word "signs" to refer to what has just transpired suggests that for the Johannine author, the resurrection appearances are included in the category of signs, as are the signs in Jesus' public ministry. These next verses are what I have called the "first ending," with which we began our exploration of John:"Now Jesus did many other signs in the presence of his disciples, which are not written in this book. But these are written so that you may come to believe that Jesus is the Messiah, the Son of God, and that through believing you may have life in his name" (John 20:30–31).

Jesus Shows Himself Beside the Sea

The final scene of the gospel resumes the action of the narrative after the summary of the gospel's purpose. The episode functions as an epilogue or update, and deals with issues arising in the community after an earlier version was finished. It begins with an appearance in Galilee to seven disciples, some named and some unnamed. The appearance provides signs of Jesus' identity in the huge haul of fish (John 21:6), the net landed untorn with one hundred and fifty three fish (21:11), and Jesus "taking and giving" the bread and fish to them (21:13). In the series of feasts in the gospel, including Cana, the wilderness feeding, the dinner with Mary and Martha and Lazarus, and the foot-washing supper, this breakfast is the last which the gospel writes down. The fact that there *is* an epilogue is a reminder of the variety of the traditions of Jesus' appearances. Perhaps these characters who have gone back to fishing need to see Jesus again, or perhaps the Johannine community needed to hear Jesus speak among them and address Peter's martyrdom and the rumor that the beloved disciple would not die.

This story resembles the story in Luke 5:1–10 where a great catch of fish is the revelation which precedes the disciples following Jesus. Here, like the other appearances in this series, Jesus is not recognized at first. He calls the disciples "children," recalling the theme in the prologue that to all who believe he gave power to become children of God. Here they do not recognize Jesus from his voice or his fishing instructions. Only the disciple whom Jesus loved recognizes him when he sees the many fish in the net. The charcoal fire recalls that which burned in the courtyard at Peter's denial; now Peter is bringing the fish ashore in obedience to Jesus' instructions. Like the seamless garment undivided by the soldiers, the untorn net is a picture of the unity of the church. As in the Luke story, fishing is a metaphor for evangelizing, and so Peter is the successful fisher. Jesus and the disciples share a Eucharist-like meal on the beach as he did with the multitude in the wilderness. This meal reflects the centrality of the Eucharist in the ongoing life of the Johannine community.

The conversation between Jesus and Peter centers around the question, "do you love me?" As we have seen, love in the gospel is the definition of discipleship. Here Jesus instructs Peter to "feed my sheep," another image for leadership in the community, as Jesus spoke of himself as the good shepherd. In this exchange Jesus is giving Peter responsibility in the community. With respect to leadership, the epilogue is bringing the gospel more into the stream of what was becoming the dominant tradition of the developing church in which Peter held the role of leader. After Jesus predicts Peter's martyrdom, Peter asks about the fate of the other disciple. Jesus clarifies that the rumor that the beloved disciple would not die was a misunderstanding. This discussion leads some to think that the death of the disciple whom Jesus loved may have happened since the earlier version of the gospel, and the epilogue was a way of addressing this transition.

The additional appearance ends with a second conclusion. As we have said, the ending doesn't finish the gospel so much as admit that there is no end to the books that would be required to contain all Jesus' deeds.

> This is the disciple who is testifying to these things and has written them, and we know that his testimony is true. But there are also many other things that Jesus did; if every one of them were written down, I suppose that the world itself could not contain the books that would be written. (John 21:24–25)

The sequence of four appearances of Jesus illustrates the creativity of Jesus and of the community who composed this gospel. Jesus appears and is known through sight, through hearing, through touch, in a garden, in closed rooms, on the shore. The presence of the epilogue shows that Jesus appears to the community even after the narrating of his appearances had apparently ended.

When Does Easter End?

Luke's story of the ascension and Pentecost told in the Gospel of Luke and Acts tells of the ascending of Jesus to heaven and the coming down of the holy spirit from heaven at Pentecost. The church calendar originates in Luke's scheme in which the season of Easter ends after forty days. John's series of signs and deeds of Jesus at and after Easter suggest that for the Gospel of John, the Easter season—the time when Jesus shows signs, appears, and speaks—is not over, but may indeed still be going on through the work of the Paraclete and through the vision of its faithful leaders.

Conversation Becomes Flesh

We think of conversation as verbal and cerebral and of studying the Bible as primarily about talking. John's gospel has shown the interplay of seeing, hearing, witnessing, and writing and the diversity and multitudes of ways to communicate the holy.

I invite you to make this conversation flesh. You have been nourished by the sensibility and style of the Fourth Gospel. Write or tell of a sign of appearance of Jesus, an Easter story of your own. You might do this alone or as the group who has been reading John together. You might incorporate into it reflection on the history that has formed your community, and you might imagine the concrete circumstances and telling details (as John does with the charcoal fire, the fragrance of the perfume, the jar left behind) which speak of your past, present, and future. What would you be doing? What would you be eating? Who would be there? Where would you be? How would you tell the story, and what means would you use to evoke a response of recognition and of faith for those who hear it? How would tradition and innovation, memory and surprise interact in your story? Try this and see what you learn. Adapt these instructions. Come and see.

Conclusion—Not the Ending

The Gospel of John is the spiritual gospel, grounded in creation and engaging the senses of sight, hearing, and touch. Visible, material, and luminous signs convey the spiritual. What is spiritual is also practical: "So if I, your Lord and Teacher, have washed your feet, you also ought to wash one another's feet. For I have set you an example, that you also should do as I have done to you" (John 13:14–15). Authority in the community of friends derives from gifts of seeing and speaking more than from office. The believing which is the purpose and end of the gospel is not ever completely finished but lives on in faithful reading in the community of friends.

Continuing the Conversation . . .

For Easter in John, see Sandra M. Schneiders, *Written that You May Believe: Encountering Jesus in the Fourth Gospel* (New York: Crossroad, 1999, 2003).

On the relationship between John and the Gospel of Thomas, see Elaine Pagels, *Beyond Belief: The Secret Gospel of Thomas* (New York: Random House, 2003).

For Mary Magdalene in history and interpretation, see Karen L. King, *The Gospel of Mary of Magdala: Jesus and the First Woman Apostle* (Santa Rosa, CA: Polebridge Press, 2003); Jane Schaberg with Melanie Johnson-DeBaufre, *Mary Magdalene Understood* (Boston: Continuum, 2006).

ACKNOWLEDGMENTS

My conversation with Scripture is enlivened and sustained by conversation among colleagues. First, I thank the Anglican Association of Biblical Scholars for the years of stimulating discussions and friendship, especially its founding president, Michael Floyd, to Loren Crow, member of the editorial board for the series who offered suggestions for this proposal, and to its president, Ellen Bradshaw Aitken.

The students at the Episcopal Theological Seminary of the Southwest inspired this project. Reading the Gospel of John together has been a process of ongoing discovery and daily surprise. I thank them for their attention, excellent questions, their memorable sermons and creative projects, and for their inquiring and discerning hearts.

My teaching colleagues, especially Ray Pickett, Jane Patterson, John Lewis, Bill Adams, and Roger Paynter have shared ideas and responses to John's gospel. Scholars and friends, Barbara Rossing, Ellen Aitken, Jennifer Berenson Maclean, Shelly Matthews, Denise Buell, Melanie Johnson-Debaufre, Laura Nasrallah, and my doctoral advisor, Elisabeth Schüssler Fiorenza are women of authority and vision who in their various kinds of work accompany me in my vocation.

The Episcopal Church of the Good Shepherd in Austin, Texas provides my parish home as well as a sensitive and thoughtful forum for teaching. I thank the members of the parish, clergy colleagues on the staff past and present, distinguished Johannine preacher, Rhoda Montgomery, and my good friend and teacher, Charlie Cook.

I thank the staff at Morehouse Publishing for their support and guidance especially Frederick Schmidt, Debra Farrington, Nancy Fitzgerald, Ryan Masteller, and Helen McPeak who wrote the questions for conversation. Their commitment to this series has enriched the biblical conversation in parishes and encouraged scholars to offer their expertise to the questions of congregations. I thank my research assistant, Carissa Baldwin, for her patience, sense of humor, her sharp eye and keen mind.

It is through repeated family suppers that I know the presence of the Paraclete who teaches, reminds, advocates, and comforts. I thank my mother, Jane Briggs, who presided at the original suppers, and long-time family member and guest, Emily Adams. I thank Rachel, Emily, and Henry for their wisdom and laughter, and Frank for friendship, partnership, and love.

STUDY QUESTIONS

The Rev. Helen McPeak

In this intentional and creative exploration of the gospel of John, Cynthia Kittredge issues a broad welcome and invites her readers to claim a new perspective on such topics as the locus of authority, the role of women in Jesus' ministry and church, and the function of Scripture in the life of believers. Requesting of her readers wide minds capable of curiosity and close attention, Kittredge opens and explores this demanding, patient, and generous gospel that crosses over and includes while inviting relationship with a companion, advocate, and teacher.

Introduction

Before you begin, pray together for God's guidance and support in this study in which you are engaging.
- What do you hope to learn?
- Why do you engage it now?
- How will you open yourself to be changed by what God will give?

Take time to read the whole of John in one sitting. (This may take several hours; relax and enjoy.)
- What reads easily?
- Where do you stumble?
- Where do you find yourself distracted?
- What do you like about this gospel?
- With what do you struggle?

Cynthia Kittredge begins her introduction by naming the "hair-raising rhetoric of hostility toward Jesus' Jewish opponents" which has led some Christians to separate from, exclude, and judge their Jewish neighbors. (p. xv)

- What do you make of this hostility?
- What has been your experience with this separating, excluding, defining, demanding gospel?
- Where have you met John before?

Look at Kittredge's list of clues toward an expansive reading of John. (p. xvi)

- Which of these pique your curiosity?
- With which do you resonate as you seek the treasures John offers to our embattled world and divided churches?

Kittredge asserts that "interpreting the Scripture of our tradition transforms us and the world we serve." (p. xvii)

- For what transformation do you yearn?
- How do the "freedom, conviction, and faith" which characterize an Anglican approach to the Bible equip you to affect this transformation?

Kittredge acknowledges a "trust in the Spirit and in the comprehensive strength of our common worship" as context for "our inquiring and analyzing and even playing with interpretations of sacred texts." (p. xviii)

- How do these trusts "encourage your own reading and wrestling with the gospel"?
- Where have you encountered such an invitation before?
- How were you taught to approach Scripture?
- What guidance was offered you as you engaged holy writings? By whom?
- How is that serving you today?

Chapter One: John Among the Gospels, the Author(s) of John, John as History

Kittredge invites us to appreciate "the distinctiveness of John's theological and artistic perspective and (to) view the difference from the gospels of Matthew, Mark, and Luke as positive, creative tension." (p. 1)

- n What difference does it make to have a variety of gospels?
- n What has been your experience with the prayer cited on page 1?

Revisit Kittredge's description of the process of canonization on pages 2–4.

- n Is this new material for you? What further information do you need?
- n How does this knowledge of the evolution of the church's understanding of John affect your own relationship to this gospel?
- n What freedoms result? What doubts undermine?

Kittredge raises the questions, "Is it OK that there is more than one version of the story of Jesus in the Bible? Does a variety of versions somehow undermine their claim to truth?" (p. 4)

- n What truths do you know in your own life?
- n How have these truths become established?
- n What are some examples of community-accepted truths that seem strong and clear? that seem misguided in your opinion?
- n What distinguishes between these?

Consider the differences that Kittredge notes between John and the other gospels. (See pp. 5–6.)

- n What are the advantages and disadvantages of multiple perspectives within the gospel canon?

Kittredge points out John's explicit clarity of purpose: "The writing of the signs is designed to evoke belief, conversion, and transformation of those who read." (p. 7)

- n What other texts do you know of that are as explicit about their purpose?
- n How do you respond to this stated goal?

Kittredge writes, "In John to believe is to embrace God's revelation in Christ. Believing is both relational and cognitive." (p. 7)
- Explore "belief." Look it up in a dictionary.
- Articulate some of your personal experiences of believing.
- What role does belief play in your life?

Revisit Kittredge's explorations of the endings of John. (pp. 7–9) She writes that the book "ends, instead of with conclusiveness, on a surprising note of openness." (p. 8)
- How does this strengthen or weaken the gospel in its purpose of evoking belief?
- What effect does this open ending have on you?

Kittredge contrasts modern biblical scholars' approach with patristic writers' close identification of apostolic authorship with authority. (p. 9)
- How does Kittredge's explanation of the "composition history" of John satisfy you?
- What is your own experience of the activity of the Spirit in studying your community's history?

Further, Kittredge writes, "Those who cherished Jesus' words and experienced them as giving life did not have the same idea as we do that Jesus said certain things and the words stayed the same forever." (p. 12)
- What would equip you to hold more loosely to the expressions of Jesus' ministry?
- What commentary on the meaning of Jesus' death and resurrection might facilitate or support the evolution of understanding?
- How do you like this concept of "a living history"?

Kittredge explains that John is a symbolically interpreted, life-giving, multi-layered gospel which uniquely acknowledges the existence of other traditions about Jesus' deeds and signs. She says it works against the orthodox impulse for finishing and closing. (p. 14)
- How do you respond to this innovative openness?
- Explore some of the resources listed on page 15 on the issue of historicity and relationship with other gospels.

Chapter Two: Beginning at the Beginning:
the Gospel Prologue

Kittredge states that the use of the prologue in liturgy indicates that it was a self-contained summary of the gospel, a hermeneutical key to the gospel. (p. 19)

- ᵰ How have you experienced this familiar passage of Scripture before this study?
- ᵰ What meaning has it carried for you?

Read the other Christological hymns in the New Testament which Kittredge suggests. (p. 20)

- ᵰ List the elements that the prologue has in common with these and watch for those elements as you proceed with this study.
- ᵰ How is your reading of John shaped by the knowledge that it opens with a corporate expression of gratitude to God?
- ᵰ How do you claim this liturgical and celebratory beginning for yourself?

Kittredge suggests a multi-layered history of composition for John which reflects a conversation in community over a period of time. (p. 21)

- ᵰ What tensions do you hear within the theological perspectives of the text?
- ᵰ What other examples can you think of that are the product of communal work over time? What are their strengths and weaknesses?

Diagram the chiasm which Kittredge explicates as reflecting the meaning of the prologue. (p. 22) Draw it out.

- ᵰ Refer to this graphic as you proceed with this chapter of the study, noting the emphases and balances.
- ᵰ Research the role of chiasms in Scripture. What function do they serve?

Revisit the openings of the three synoptic gospels.

- ᵰ What emphases do you find there?
- ᵰ How do they differ from John?
- ᵰ Where do you find specific details? divine communication? clear narratives? ancient prophecies? transcendent perspectives?
- ᵰ Do you resonate with any particular presentation? Why?

Kittredge cites scholars of religion, "early Christians found in the Jewish myth of Wisdom as creative force and mediator between God and human a compelling way to understand Jesus' ministry, crucifixion, and resurrection." She reminds us that hearing the allusions of Wisdom in the gospel "recalls and highlights many traditional ways of imagining the divine as a woman and emphasizes the close kinship between Jesus/Logos/Wisdom and the creation/cosmos/world." (p. 24)

- Read the Wisdom texts Kittredge lists, comparing and contrasting the figures of Wisdom and Jesus.
- What details grab your attention as you explore the Logos?

What does Kittredge name as the tragedy which produces so much of the energy of the gospel?

- Review her offered interpretations. (See p. 26.)
- What function is served by "the kinship of Logos with the creation of all things"?
- Explore that rejection and kinship using the resources which Kittredge offers for continuing the conversation on page 31.

Kittredge names Jesus' lack of success in the section Raymond Brown calls "the Book of Signs." (p. 28)

- How does she explain this?
- What does Kittredge say is illustrated in the second section, Brown's "Book of Glory"?
- What is the empowerment offered? (p. 28)

In exploring the fourth and final stanza of the prologue, Kittredge points out that the word "flesh" (*sarx*), used to express the doctrine of the incarnation, has graphic and realistic connotations (pp. 28–29).

- What are the implications of this word choice?

Continuing in this vein, explore the profound implications of "to tent," *skenao*.

- Where else in the Scripture are these Greek words used?
- How do you experience "realized eschatology," the theological idea of the ongoing presence of God with us?
- What are the implications of God's choosing to dwell with us? How does this affect your actions in the world?

Chapter Three: Signs in the Gospel and Gospel as Sign

Kittredge writes, "All the gospels are persuasive religious literature which seeks to communicate the character and import of Jesus, the gospel's subject and hero." (p. 33) She explains the way John highlights this communicative function by calling Jesus' mighty deeds "signs."

- Revisit her explanation of the word "sign," *semeion*.
- What do signs communicate?
- How do they differ from sacraments in John?

In what ways do John's signs' "far-ranging and rich connotations" help us to appreciate "the neglected dimensions of the sacrament of the eucharist"?

- Where/how do wilderness feeding and farewell footwashing direct our focus?
- What is unique in this focus?

Revisit Kittredge's list of signs in John's story of Jesus' public ministry (p. 34) and the discussion of the complexity of these revelations of the divine. Kittredge writes, "the signs are not communicating something exciting about the near future, but something real and true about the present." (p. 35)

- What do the multi-layered and symbolic qualities of those evolved stories reveal to us about God?

Kittredge asserts, "Truths about God are not straightforwardly accessible, but must be communicated by indirect means, a medium that can be misunderstood as easily as comprehended." (p. 36) She points out that these signs are enigmatic, concealing and revealing, dividing as well as uniting: "Characters respond to signs in positive, negative, and ambivalent ways."

- How is this explained in the gospel of John?
- How do you experience this reality in your own life and that of your community?
- Where is belief evoked in conversation? Where undermined? What determines the difference?

Kittredge stresses two points about signs in John in response to common misunderstandings. (See pp. 36–37.)

- What are the two points?
- What is the attitude of the gospel toward "signs faith" (faith based on signs)?
- In what ways is the glory of God repeatedly revealed in John?
- What does Kittredge state one must grasp as the key to doing justice to the expansive foundation of this gospel? (p. 37)?

Kittredge comments on the particular details and odd sequence of the story of Jesus' first sign at the wedding at Cana.

- How do these details communicate more symbolically than realistically?
- How would you respond to her "more promising questions" on page 39?
- Are you comfortable trusting the Logos within you to be acting as you wonder about these responses? Why or why not?

Revisit Kittredge's comments regarding the symbolism of the marriage feast.

- Explore this image further, both in scholarly resources and in the experience of your study group.
- Look up "consummation" in a dictionary. How does this resonate?
- Why are consummation and the participation of Jesus and his friends important themes in the story of this first sign?
- What good news is being proclaimed?

Kittredge writes of the feeding and walking on water following the sermon, "Jesus demands more and more specific beliefs and practices, and appears to lose people in the process." (p. 43)

- What reasons does she give for this shift?
- What is the effect on you of this story of divine plenty and generosity?
- In what ways do you find "its non-conformity . . . initially disorienting, but ultimately enriching"? (p. 45)

Reread John 6:16–21 in which Jesus comforts the disciples with the first of the great "I am" statements of the gospel.

- How do you respond to Kittredge's invitation to imagine what the predicate might be in an alternative midrash on the sea walking? (See p. 45.)
- What observations does she make about the emphases of other "I am" speeches in John?

As you review this chapter of Kittredge's study, what broad themes reveal themselves?

- Have the signs John tells supported your belief in the life of Jesus?
- So what? How will you behave differently for having thought about this?

Chapter Four: Your Father the Devil: Jews and Jewish Tradition in John

In this chapter, Kittredge explores the dynamics of hate and love in John.

- How do you respond to her citing another scholar to the effect of "while for some people the gospel of John is the gospel of love, for some readers, it might be called the gospel of hate." (p. 49)?
- Can you "imagine hearing the text as others do, with the ears of Jewish readers or those outside the circle of belief"? How is that for you?
- What do you do with the gospel's portrayal of "sharp and irreconcilable opposition between those who believe and those who do not, between Jesus and 'the world.'" (p. 51)? How does the language of opposition affect you?

As baptized Christians, we promise to seek and serve Christ in all persons. Kittredge calls us to task: "The sins committed in the name of these texts by our Christian ancestors make it necessary for us to struggle with the ethical problems poses by such harsh and uncompromising language." (p. 52)

- What will you do in response to this invitation "to try to understand the language of hate and to be in active and vigorous conversation with it"?

Articulate "the historical situation of the Johannine community in relationship with its Jewish neighbors at the time of the writing of the gospel." (p. 52)

- Using outside resources, expand your knowledge of that historical situation.
- What traumatic rift has been theorized?
- What feelings are reflected in the language of enmity in the gospel?
- Explore some of the extremes to which this dualism led.

Kittredge asserts, "the gospel of John's anti-Judaism is the most disruptive element to an expansive reading." (p. 54)

- What is required, according to Kittredge, to help us find respectful ways to be in dialogue with faithful Jews?

Read John 11:1–46 about the death and raising of Lazarus.

- In what ways do the actions of the neighbors of Martha and Mary during this time of grief belie the hateful dualism Kittredge discusses?
- What is the effect on Martha and Mary?
- What is the effect on the community?

Read John 4:5–42 about Jesus' encounter with the Samaritan woman. Kittredge says that this passage provides "a paradigm or icon for the expansive arc of the gospel and to a great extent, counteracts the rigidity of its black and white outlook." (pp. 57–58) She addresses it "not as a realistic report of an episode during Jesus' lifetime, but a highly structured, developed version enriched by the experience of the Johannine community with Samaritan mission, women apostolic leaders, and discrimination." (p. 58) Revisit Kittredge's discussion of the story with its racy connotations of sex, marriage, religion, prostitution, and foreigners. In the midst of it all is a minority woman who pushes back on Jesus' authority in ways both literal and beyond.

- What role does this dialogue play in eliciting faith? (See p. 60.)
- What is the effect of Jesus' self-revelation on the Samaritan woman?
- What does Kittredge suggest she represents in this gospel?
- In what ways have you been brought to Jesus' presence by the testimony of others?

◻ What direct experience of Jesus invites you towards deeper levels of belief?

Kittredge writes of the reality of the language of hate and love in the gospel of John. She allows that this Samaritan heroine does not necessarily contradict the anti-Jewish perspective of the gospel as a whole. However, Kittredge goes beyond that.

◻ What guidance does Kittredge offer towards discovering the gospel's assertion of Christ's incarnation and his involvement with the creation of all things?

◻ Are you convinced? What more would you like to know?

Chapter Five: The Beloved Community: Leadership among the Disciples Whom Jesus Loves

Kittredge invites us to "picture (the Last Supper as you know it) askew, with its most familiar element missing, the institution of the eucharist, and in its place, another rite, followed by hours of teaching which spin and weave and expand the significance of that rite and reflect back upon the meaning of Jesus' encounters during his encampment in the world." (p. 65)

◻ How does that work for you?

◻ Where is it comfortable?

◻ Where is this imagined image a challenge to you?

Read John 13–17 about the last supper and sermon.

◻ Do some exegesis on foot washing in first century Mediterranean culture: When was it done? By whom? What did it represent?

◻ What has been your own experience of foot washing?

◻ What does Kittredge suggest is the purpose of the foot washing in John?

Revisit Kittredge's discussion of friendship as Jesus' ministry in John. (pp. 68–70)

◻ What is the etymology of "friendship"? Check out an etymological dictionary and see what you find.

◻ Compare these ideas with your own experiences and observations of friendship. Where do you experience groups that are "intimate, but not elite"?

Kittredge comments, "It is intriguing to reflect on the meaning of this division (between the narration of deeds of public ministry in the Book of Signs and the more intimate teaching of the community of the beloved disciples) in the gospel." (p. 69)

- Explore this division further.
- What do you note about the public versus the private ministry accounts?
- Which of the explanations Kittredge offers fits well for you?

Research *meno*.

- In what other contexts is this verb used? with what connotations?
- Where else do you find similar activity in the Scripture? in your lived reality?

Kittredge writes, "When read in its place in the gospel of John, the story eloquently proclaims Mary's authority and leadership in the memory of this community." (p. 72)

- Look again at the distinctions from other gospels that Kittredge highlights for us.
- How is this unique role for Mary familiar?
- How does it expand your thinking?

In her explanations of the role of "the beloved disciple," Kittredge presents particular parallels and uniquenesses in the role. (See pp. 72–74.)

- Upon what does Kittredge see leadership in John as primarily based?
- What roles do seeing and witnessing have in this leadership?
- Why is the anonymity of "the beloved disciple" important in John?

Kittredge notes pastoral and reassuring dimensions as well as legal connotations of the Paraclete, the Advocate. (p. 75)

- In what ways does the presence of the Paraclete alleviate the problem of leadership succession in John?
- What will the vital and active presence of the Paraclete do in the community?
- How is the ongoing quality of the Spirit's presence expressed and expected in John? in your own community?

Kittredge writes of the specific and varied activities of "the beloved disciple" and yet this person remains nameless. (p. 76)

- ⌐ What are the implications of the namelessness of the disciple about whom the memory of the community centers?
- ⌐ What invitation is effected in this naming void?

Kittredge states, "the Johannine community who authored this gospel experienced the vigorous activity of the Paraclete in their midst." (p. 77)

- ⌐ In what ways does your community experience and claim the vigorous activity of the Paraclete in your midst?
- ⌐ How is your vision of Jesus the medium through which people come to belief?

Chapter Six: Multiple Modes of Knowing: Easter in John

Reread John 19:31 to the end. Kittredge asserts that the gospel message can only be properly spoken through the complexity, the intricacy, and the playfulness John models. (p. 79) John is full of narratives whose meanings far outrun their surface level, while still depending upon material realities as they meander along invitingly. Again, "the paradox and mystery and elusiveness of the Word coming into the world can be expressed in no other way." (p. 80)

- ⌐ How do you respond to this "patient and generous" presentation of gospel truth?
- ⌐ What metaphors come to mind for the necessity of this indirect approach to the paradox, mystery, and elusiveness of the Word coming into the world?
- ⌐ Why must it be so?
- ⌐ How do the repetition and variation which the gospel employs support the goal of calling forth belief?

Kittredge writes that John, like all the gospels, is written in the light of Easter. (p. 80)

- ⌐ What does she mean by this?
- ⌐ In what ways are you reading John now in the light of Easter? What is more clear? What shadows are cast?
- ⌐ In what ways do you still seek to know "the explosive experience of resurrection"?

Kittredge notes that "only in John is Jesus buried in a garden." (p. 82)

- Explore the imagery of gardens in Scripture.
- Why is it important that John sets Jesus' burial in a garden?
- What do gardens represent in your own life?

Review Kittredge's discussion of Mary coming to the tomb. (p. 82)

- How do you respond to Kittredge's invitation "to let go of the image of Mary, the repentant and reformed sinner, coming in the dark to the tomb on the first day of the week"?
- How does John use Mary's incomplete understanding of the truth to invite your belief in Jesus?
- What elements of their interaction allow Mary to know Jesus? What allows this shift from misunderstanding to communion?
- Where are you given the opportunity to offer these elements in your own ministry?

Kittredge explores Jesus' instructions not to hold on to him on page 84.

- What interpretation of this instruction resonates best with the whole of John?
- To where does Jesus redirect Mary's attention, according to Kittredge?
- Into what role does this place Mary?
- What implications does Jesus' instruction have for our attention today?
- Where do you find effective leadership in the Church in our own times?

Kittredge comments that "unlike the Lukan story of the giving of the Spirit at Pentecost, this is a quiet affair, emphasizing soft wind and not fire." (Acts 2:1–13). (pp. 86–87)

- What effect does this gentleness have on the reader?
- How is it in keeping with John's style throughout the gospel?

Check out Kittredge's suggestions of better names for Thomas. (p. 87)

- What else do you know of Thomas? (See John 11:16 and 14:5.)
- What does Jesus offer Thomas in response to his demands?
- What experience do you need to believe?

John 20:31 states that "these (signs) are written so that you may come to believe that Jesus is the Messiah, the Son of God, and that through believing you may have life in his name."

- What does life in Jesus' name look like?
- How do you recognize it?

In recounting the variety of traditions of Jesus' appearances, John includes one more feast after the summary of the gospel's purpose.

- To what metaphors does Kittredge call the readers' attention?
- What emphasis is reflected for the ongoing life of the Johannine community?
- How does this account "bring the gospel more into the stream of what was becoming the dominant tradition of the developing church in which Peter held the role of leader"? (p. 90)

Kittredge reminds her readers that "for the gospel of John, the Easter season, the time when Jesus shows signs, appears, speaks, is not over, but may indeed still be going on through the work of the Paraclete and through the vision of its faithful leaders." (p. 91)

- So what?!
- In what ways do you participate in the ongoing Easter season?

Noticing "the diversity and multitudes of ways to communicate the holy," Kittredge invites us to enflesh this conversation.

- Go there. Follow her suggestions on page 91 for imagining the concrete circumstances and telling details which speak of your past, present, and future. Adapt her instructions to fit your particular situation. What do you find?
- What difference does it make that you have studied this expansive and promising gospel? How have your prayers at the opening of this study been answered? Whom will you tell?

The Rev. Helen McPeak serves as Priest Associate at the Episcopal Church of the Epiphany in Henderson, NV. Her roles as wife and mother bring her into contact with multiple manifestations of God's friendship and she is joyfully surprised by the expansive and feminine presence of the Divine.

NOTES

Introduction to the Series

1. David F. Ford, "The Bible, the World, and the Church I," in *The Report of the Lambeth Conference 1998* (ed. J. Mark Dyer et al.; Harrisburg, Pa.: Morehouse Publishing, 1999), 332.
2. "The Anglican Church has always existed in a context of rival ways of ordering the Church. On the one hand it has refused an authoritarian solution, where one central authority holds out the attractive possibility of getting rid of the messiness of debate, dissent, and rival interpretations of Scripture by pronouncements and commands that permit no argument. On the other hand, it has resisted the sort of diversity in which everyone is free to do according to their own interpretation and conscience, and no one is ultimately accountable to anyone else" (Ford, 367).

Chapter One: John Among the Gospels: Orienting John in History and Canon

3. Elaine H. Pagels, *The Johannine Gospel in Gnostic Exegesis: Heracleon's Commentary on John*, Society of Biblical Literature Monograph Series 17 (Nashville: Abingdon, 1973).
4. Elaine H. Pagels, *Beyond Belief: The Secret Gospel of Thomas* (New York: Random House, 2003).
5. Irenaeus, *Against Heresies*, 11.8, in Cyril C. Richardson, ed., *Early Christian Fathers*, vol. 1, Library of Christian Classics (Philadelphia: Westminster, 1953), 382.
6. All biblical quotations are from the New Revised Standard Version unless otherwise noted.
7. The definition of belief is treated in many works on John. For a particularly clear and practical discussion of believing and of implications for preaching, see Robert Kysar, *Preaching John* (Minneapolis: Fortress, 2002), 62–66.

8. Irenaeus, *Against Heresies,* 370.

9. Rudolf Bultmann, Raymond Brown, *The Community of the Beloved Disciple* (New York: Paulist Press, 1979).

10. Steven L. Davies, *The New Testament: A Contemporary Introduction* (San Francisco: Harper and Row, 1988).

11. Eusebius, *The History of the Church from Christ to Constantine,* trans. G. A. Williamson (London: Penguin Books, 1989), 254–55 (VI.14.7).

Chapter Two: Beginning at the Beginning: The Gospel Prologue

12. Rudolf Bultmann, The Gospel of John, *The Gospel of John: A Commentary* (Philadelphia: Westminster, 1971).

13. R. Alan Culpepper, *The Gospel and Letters of John* (Nashville: Abingdon, 1998).

14. See the reconstructions in Raymond Brown, 3–4. Sharon H. Ringe, *Wisdom's Friends: Community and Christology in the Fourth Gospel* (Louisville: Westminster, 1999), 46–63. R. Alan Culpepper, *The Gospel and Letters of John* (Nashville: Abingdon, 1998), 113–114.

15. Raymond Brown, *The Gospel According to John, Anchor Bible Commentary* (New York: Doubleday, 1966), 33. Sharon H. Ringe, *Wisdom's Friends: Community and Christology in the Fourth Gospel* (Louisville: Westminster John Knox, 1999), 51–52.

Chapter Three: Mighty Works: Signs in the Gospel and the Gospel as Sign

16. Robert T. Fortna, *Fourth Gospel and its Predecessor: From Narrative Source to Present Gospel* (Philadelphia: Fortress, 1988).

Chapter Four: Your Father the Devil: Jews and Jewish Tradition in John

17. Adele Reinhartz, *Befriending the Beloved Disciple: A Jewish Reading of the Gospel of John* (New York: Continuum, 2001), 25.

18. For a fine treatment of the relationship between Christian anti-Judaism and anti-Semitism, see James Carroll, *Constantine's Sword: The Church and the Jews: A History* (Boston: Houghton Mifflin, 2001).

19. Alan F. Segal, *Rebecca's Children: Judaism and Christianity in the Roman World* (Cambridge: Harvard University Press, 1986), 163–81.

20. Reinhartz, *Befriending the Beloved Disciple,* 37–53.

21. Wayne Meeks, "The Man from Heaven in Johannine Sectarianism." *Journal of Biblical Literature* 91 (1972): 44–72.
22. Reinhartz, *Befriending the Beloved Disciple*, 43–48.
23. Sandra M. Schneiders, *Written that You May Believe* (New York: Crossroad, 1999, 2003), 178.
24. Ibid., 179–183.

Chapter Five: The Beloved Community: Leadership among the Disciples Whom Jesus Loves

25. Ringe, *Wisdom's Friends*, 69–74.
26. For a summary of scholarly efforts to determine the identity of the beloved disciple and an eloquent argument for the gospel's intentional mystification of the character's identity, see Harold W. Attridge, "The Restless Quest for the Beloved Disciple" in David H. Warren, Ann Graham Brock, and David W. Pao, eds., *Early Christian Voices in Texts, Traditions, and Symbols: Essays in Honor of François Bovon, Biblical Interpretation Series* 66 (Leiden: Brill, 2003), 71–80.
27. Andrew T. Lincoln, *Truth on Trial: The Lawsuit Motif in the Fourth Gospel* (Peabody, MA: Hendrickson, 2000).

Chapter Six: Multiple Modes of Knowing: Easter in John

28. Sandra Schneiders argues that what the beloved disciple sees is Jesus' face veil as a sign of Jesus' resurrection, *Written that You May Believe*, 207–208.
29. Ibid., 219–221.
30. Jane Schaberg, *The Resurrection of Mary Magdalene: Legends, Apocrypha, and the Christian Testament* (New York: Continuum, 2002); Jane Schaberg with Melanie Johnson-DeBaufre, *Mary Magdalene Understood* (Boston: Continuum, 2006).
31. Elaine Pagels, *Belief: The Secret Gospel of Thomas* (New York: Random House, 2003); Karen L. King, *The Gospel of Mary of Magdala: Jesus and the First Woman Apostle* (Santa Rosa, CA: Polebridge Press, 2003).

FURTHER READING

As with all books of the New Testament, the literature on John is extensive and fascinating. The following books have particularly influenced this expansive reading of John. They are accessible and their perspectives will lead you into your own areas of investigation in the Fourth Gospel.

Brown, Raymond. *The Gospel According to John.* Anchor Bible. New York: Doubleday, 1966–70. Raymond Brown's two volume commentary on John is thorough and dense. It is a good place to begin for detailed answered to many questions about the text and its history.

Culpepper, R. Alan. *The Gospel and Letters of John.* Interpreting Biblical Texts. Nashville: Abingdon, 1998. Alan Culpepper's readable commentary includes a thoughtful discussion of the theological challenges of reading John's gospel.

Schneiders, Sandra M. *Written That You May Believe: Encountering Jesus in the Fourth Gospel.* New York: Crossroad, 1999, 2003. Sandra Schneiders's brilliant essays on the Fourth Gospel convey the sacramental quality of the text and offer persuasive arguments for the centrality of women as representative characters in the gospel.

Countryman, L. William. *The Mystical Way in the Fourth Gospel: Crossing Over in God.* Valley Forge, PA: Trinity Press, 1994. The exploration of John by William Countryman attends to the spiritual and mystical dimensions of the gospel. As the volumes in this series, his work builds bridges between scholarship and readers of Scripture in the church.

Ringe, Sharon. *Wisdom's Friends: Community and Christology in the Fourth Gospel.* Louisville, KY: Westminster John Knox Press, 1999. Sharon Ringe traces the motifs of Wisdom and Friendship in the gospel and draws out their theological implications.

ABOUT THE AUTHOR

Cynthia Briggs Kittredge is an Episcopal priest and Associate Professor of New Testament at the Episcopal Theological Seminary of the Southwest in Austin, Texas. Ordained in 1984, she has served parishes in Massachusetts and now assists at the Episcopal Church of the Good Shepherd in Austin, Texas. Before coming to the Seminary of the Southwest in 1999, she taught at the College of the Holy Cross and Harvard Divinity School.

Cynthia received her B.A. in Religion and English from Williams College. She studied for the ministry at Harvard Divinity School where she earned her M.Div. She returned to Harvard Divinity School where she received the Th.M. in 1989 and the Th.D. in 1996. Her other publications are *Community and Authority: The Rhetoric of Obedience in the Pauline Tradition* and *Walk in the Ways of Wisdom: Essays in Honor of Elisabeth Schüssler Fiorenza.* She has contributed to the introduction and notes to Hebrews in the New Oxford Annotated Bible. She is Chair of the Paul and Politics Group of the Society of Biblical Literature and serves on the Board of the Evangelical Education Society of the Episcopal Church.

Cynthia and her husband, Frank D. Kittredge Jr., have two children in college, Rachel and Emily, and one, Henry, at home in Austin.

ALSO IN THE ANGLICAN ASSOCIATION OF BIBLICAL SCHOLARS STUDY SERIES

Conversations with Scripture:
REVELATION

"If ever theological scholarship met the laity with grace and respect, it is here in this volume. . . . I was charmed; I was instructed; I was deeply, deeply comforted by this book. Buy it, read it, and then take it to your heart for understanding."
—Phyllis Tickle, compiler, *The Divine Hours*

"This is an important start to a most welcome series. Schmidt is a gracious and experienced teacher. He knows what false expectations his readers are likely to bring to the reading of Revelation, and offers just what we need for an encounter with the book that is honest to the text and to ourselves. . . . Schmidt's book will be widely used; and deserves to be."
—Robin Griffin-Jones, author of *The Gospel According to Paul: The Creative Genius Who Brought Jesus to the World*

MOREHOUSE PUBLISHING

Morehouse books are available from Episcopal and online booksellers, or directly from the publisher at 800-242-1918 or online at www.churchpublishing.org.

ALSO IN THE ANGLICAN ASSOCIATION OF BIBLICAL SCHOLARS STUDY SERIES

**Conversations with Scripture:
THE LAW**

"Kevin Wilson's introductory exposition of biblical Law is a must read. Unusually wide-ranging and broadly informative for a book of its size, it is jam-packed with information about the Torah's commandments, sacrifices, rituals, and theology. Wilson works hard to explain clearly how we hear God's Word today in these texts of the Law."
—Stephen L. Cook, Department of Old Testament, Virginia
   Theological Seminary

"Fresh insights into the meaning of the Law—and how Exodus and Leviticus provide guidelines for ethical behavior that helped shape a covenant community."
—*Diocesan Dialogue*, September 2006

"This addition to the series breaks new ground. This is a gem for adult education."
—*The Living Church*, November 2006

MOREHOUSE PUBLISHING

Morehouse books are available from Episcopal and online booksellers, or directly from the publisher at 800-242-1918 or online at www.churchpublishing.org.

ALSO IN THE ANGLICAN ASSOCIATION OF BIBLICAL SCHOLARS STUDY SERIES

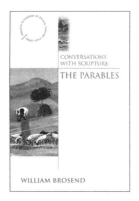

Conversations with Scripture:
THE PARABLES

The parables are vivid, rich, arresting stories that make us think, and teach us lessons about our relationship with God and others. From talents to mustard seeds, from shepherds to Samaritans, William Brosend shows how Jesus used common reference points to teach important truths.

MOREHOUSE PUBLISHING

Morehouse books are available from Episcopal and online booksellers, or directly from the publisher at 800-242-1918 or online at www.churchpublishing.org.